LOUIS ARMSTRONG, BLUES MUSIC, AND THE ARTISTIC, POLITICAL, AND PHILOSOPHICAL DEBATE DURING THE HARLEM RENAISSANCE

DR. MICHAEL DECUIR

Copyright © 2023 Dr. Michael Decuir.

All rights reserved. No part of this book may be reproduced, stored, or transmitted by any means—whether auditory, graphic, mechanical, or electronic—without written permission of both publisher and author, except in the case of brief excerpts used in critical articles and reviews. Unauthorized reproduction of any part of this work is illegal and is punishable by law.

ISBN: 979-8-89031-396-6 (sc)
ISBN: 979-8-89031-397-3 (hc)
ISBN: 979-8-89031-398-0 (e)

Because of the dynamic nature of the Internet, any web addresses or links contained in this book may have changed since publication and may no longer be valid. The views expressed in this work are solely those of the author and do not necessarily reflect the views of the publisher, and the publisher hereby disclaims any responsibility for them.

One Galleria Blvd., Suite 1900, Metairie, LA 70001
(504) 702-6708

CONTENTS

Introduction vii

Chapter 1 Armstrong's and the Period's Origins 1

Chapter 2 The Precursors to "Texas Moaner Blues"
           and Armstrong's Early Years 25

Chapter 3 Louis Armstrong, W. E. B. Du Bois, and the
           Business of Blues Music During the Harlem
           Renaissance 41

Chapter 4 Agitate or Create: the Dilemma of Black Arts
           During the Harlem Renaissance 64

Chapter 5 Louis Armstrong and Blues Music's Impact as a
           Functional Art During the Harlem Renaissance 104

Chapter 6 Louis Armstrong, the New Negro Philosophy,
           and Blues Music in American Culture 137

Chapter 7 Coda 177

Appendix A: Significant Louis Armstrong Recordings as a
            Band Leader 1925–1930 189

Appendix B: Significant Louis Armstrong Recordings as a
            Sideman 1923–1930 192

Bibliography 198

About the Author 211

LIST OF FIGURES

Figure 1. Louis Armstrong's artistic contributions and interrelated artistic, political, and philosophical events, 1923–1930 2

Figure 2. Louis Armstrong's, Sidney Bechet's, and Charles Irvis's rendition of "Texas Moaner Blues" 38

Figure 3. Louis Armstrong's opening fanfare to "West End Blues" 87

Figure 4. Louis Armstrong's improvised solo in *West End Blues* 94

INTRODUCTION

I argue in this research that the performing, literary, and visual arts present during the period known as the Harlem Renaissance did not evolve in a vacuum. Just as in other documented cultural or historical periods, sources of said artistic inspirations must be traced. Particularly when the historical record thus far has been largely distorted or untold. Therefore, my pleasurable task was to trace the West African influences on the enslaved culture (music, behaviors, mores, etc.) in New Orleans and thus Louis Armstrong's art and sub-sequently the nuanced discussion of the period considered here. Like Armstrong, I was born and came of age in a region, New Orleans, fraught with vestiges of West African culture promulgated by the descendants of the enslaved. Life in the Southern American apartheid system was confusing at best and painful at worst. Often, the dominant culture welcomes glimpses of Africanisms when we gather or celebrate funerals in the New Orleans-Ewe-Ibo behaviors. However, the early years of New Orleans was a manifestation and perpetuation of Jean Baptiste Bienville's and other early slaveholders' (who were motivated by monetary greed) colonial land-owner aspirations and what historian Gwendolyn Mildo Hall called an "Anglophone orientation." The slaveholders and European colonists embraced a persistent myth in the western hemisphere that the descendants of the enslaved Africans and the aboriginal population are intellectually incapable of contributing to European culture beyond an imitative role and consequently the beneficiaries of Western civilization culture taught or assimilated. The myth served as the aquifer for the resistance to efforts to gain constitutional rights denied to people of color, including the primary subject of this research, Louis Armstrong.

I came of age during the segregation-integration transition years in New Orleans and benefitted from teachers who recognized that, contrary to the opinion of many of the slaveholders' descendants and lawmakers, my classmates and I possessed intellect and talents that were as good as or better than any other students. They were intelligent and prideful enough to supplement our textbooks, which were devoid of any African American contributions to history and culture with examples of literary, performing, and visual arts by the likes of Paul Lawrence Dunbar, Louis Armstrong, and Aaron Douglas. The latter two were salient contributors to the Harlem Renaissance. Learning of these artists as well as an existential awareness of the greatness of Africa, particularly the nation-states that predated Christopher Columbus's actions in the western hemi-phere by hundreds of years. Much of the first chapter is dedicated to the subsequent West African sources of the period's arts, politics, and philosophy.

Poignantly, this writer's editing and corrections are simultaneous with the contemporaneous lynching incidents involving George Floyd, Ahmaud Arbery, and Breonna Taylor. Additionally, many are contemporaneously mourning the death of Civil Rights Icon John Lewis. One of Lewis's many contributions to freedom and recognition of the humanity in all people Americans was his courageous attempt to peacefully protest the perpetual disenfranchisement of Black Americans in the South, particularly Selma AL. Notably, Lewis and others were beaten after crossing the Edmond Pettus Bridge and attempting to collectively walk to the state's capitol, Montgomery. It has arguably become one of the signature events in Lewis's storied history and the history of the fight for freedom in this country. Like his expressed outrage a decade earlier at Arkansas Governor Forbes's attempts to block the integration of Central High School in Little Rock, Armstrong responded to the Selma terrorist attack, "They would have beaten Jesus if he was Black and marched."[1] It is this writer's wish that the recent

---

[1] *Jet Magazine*, March 25, 1965, 63.

events mentioned here are placed in the historical context of the period (Harlem Renaissance) considered here and beyond. Additionally, I am fascinated with the popularity particularly among young Black Americans with the "Black Panther" movies. I witnessed with glee the sold-out theaters. On so many levels, Black theater goers seemed to yearn the historical knowledge presented in a futuristic setting. I enjoyed the plot's parallels to West African cultural behaviors that were juxtaposed with technological innovations.

My research explores the efforts of Ida B. Wells and her valiant fight to bring the terrorist attacks on Black Americans to the public's awareness and put an end to the practice through legislative means. At the time of this writing, the nation is currently experiencing what Langston Hughes referred to in his poem, "A Dream Deferred," an explosion. The contemporaneous (summer 2020) expressions of outrage over police terrorist acts parallel the summer 1919 and beyond. Indeed, the institution of slavery has inspired a perpetual lynching atmosphere, and the consequential racist institutions cannot be eradicated without a thorough examination of the historical reasons why. Historically, there was a concerted, but futile effort to pass an anti-lynching bill during the period considered here. Currently, anti-lynching legislation named for George Floyd is meeting a similar fate. In many ways, incidents of institutional and systemic racism were contributing factors to the period considered in this research. For example, amid failing efforts to find a white physician willing to treat his ill infant son, W. E. B. Du Bois saw the severed fingers of a lynched man for sale in an Atlanta storefront. Louis Armstrong was almost attacked when white terrorists went on a rampage after Jack Johnson's defeat of Jim Jefferies. Indeed, over fifty innocent people were terrorized after Johnson's victory.

America has a history of schizophrenic appropriation of Black art or talent. In some cases, this nation only seeks to reward the aesthetic pleasure of Black entertainment. Such was the case during the period considered here and beyond. Armstrong was aware that many of the consumers of his performance art would otherwise endorse the denial of constitutional rights. Similarly, I theorize that George Floyd's murderers would likely and enthusiastically cheer for him to score touchdowns for the state's university or professional teams. Armstrong's warmth, stage presence, and sense of hospitality were integral to his art. Armstrong was aware of the ramifications of his 1926 recording of "Black and Blue."

In 1957, he made a point to perform it for an audience in Ghana that included the new nation's future president, Kwame Nkrumah.

Armstrong recognized and responded publicly to the reactionary actions against Civil Rights protests. The parallels here are both clear and poignant. Decades earlier, specifically, W.E.B. Du Bois and others were arguing for the removal of the colonial occupation in West Africa and the vestiges of the genocidal behaviors resulting from the Berlin Conference when Armstrong was developing his craft in New Orleans and Chicago. Decades later, he performed for and witnessed the rise of one of the continent's greatest leaders at the dawn of the elimination of colonial control. Some would pay to hear "Blind" Willie Johnson but refuse to live next door to him.

One of this nation's most salient contributors to American music is Louis Armstrong. Biographers and musicologists have successfully researched and published his or her roles in shifting America's cultural gift to the world, jazz music, from an ensemble-focused performing art to an emphasis on the individual soloist during the period considered here. It is important to note that he was not the only artist significantly contributing to the Harlem Renaissance. For example, the contributions of Edward "Duke" Ellington, Thomas Wright "Fats" Waller, Eubie Blake, and Fletcher Henderson are significant to the period's performing art. To this end, Louis Armstrong's improvisational approach to blues music on recordings and live performances as a sideman and as the lead artist between 1923 and 1930 sets him apart from other contributors. However, in much of the literature written about the cultural achievements of the Harlem Renaissance, the artistic contributions of Louis Armstrong are underestimated and under-researched. Armstrong's creative choices between the years 1923 and 1930 infinitely influenced and inspired the literary, performing, and visual arts as well as the political and philosophical debate during the Harlem Renaissance (see Figure 1). Subsequently, there were interrelatedness and cross influences between the period's contributing entities. Armstrong's presence on blues and jazz recordings as well as his public performances in Chicago with Joe "King" Oliver, in New York with the Fletcher Henderson Orchestra, and his own Hot Five and Hot Seven bands helped fuel a rise in the popularity of blues and jazz music. The period's performing art was the source of inspiration to many of the period's literary, performing, and visual artists.

Armstrong's childhood and adolescent New Orleans was fraught with Africanisms, from the food to the music. Most of the region's slave populations (one to two generations removed) were directly from specific regions and peoples in West Africa. They brought with them a variety of languages, diet, belief systems, all with physical movement limited. The popularity of the arts mentioned above inspired a philosophical debate regarding the brought existence and purpose of the period's arts and leading figures such as W. E. B. Du Bois, Alain Locke, Langston Hughes, and George Schuyler led the discussion. This research shall explore the debate in the context of Theodor Adorno's theories regarding music, as expressed in *On Popular Music*. Adorno's insight into the artistic process in the art's creator/consumer paradigm is invaluable. Additionally, W. E. B. Du Bois's (art is propaganda and should be used to agitate for a political and social change) 1926 speech to the National Association for the Advancement of Colored People titled "The Criteria of Negro Art" shall serve as the context for the role of the period's art.

In contrast, Alain Locke theorized two years later in an essay titled "Art or Propaganda" that Black artists should acquiesce to Eurocentric models to gain acceptance from the dominant culture. This research will explore opposing theories expressed by George Schuyler in "The Negro Art-Hokum" and Langston Hughes's "The Negro Artist and the Racial Mountain." Schuyler believed that not only is African American art nonexistent, but the individuals extolling the virtues of such art are harmful to progress in post-World War I America. Hughes, on the other hand, adopted an opposing position, arguing that African American artists should proudly use the proclivities of life in America as a source of their art. This research also places an analysis of Hughes's essay mentioned above and Armstrong's creative choices (detailed in a music transcription) in "West End Blues" in the context of Paulo Freire's *Fear of Freedom* theory espoused in his publication, *Pedagogy of the Oppressed*. Both, in their respective mediums codified (albeit forty-five years earlier) Freire's position on removing the shackles of oppression. The transcriptions and corresponding analyses will show that the act of recognizing the source(s) of one's problems and prescribing solutions are at the heart of blues music.

Words could never express what it means to be born and come of age in New Orleans. I was blessed with great teachers and mentors particularly during the challenging 1960s and 1970s. New Orleans has allowed me to know and perform with some of the greatest of God's creations, New Orleans musicians. The late Edward "Kidd" Jordan continues to inspire me. I will always cherish the time I spent with him as a student and mentee. He embodied Paulo Freire's concept of an artist ridding him or herself of the "fear of freedom." Special thanks to all my teachers. Especially my alma mater, Clark Atlanta University's Dr. Timothy Askew for encouraging and believing in my efforts. Thank you to the Hogan Jazz Archives and the Amistad Research Center on the campus of Tulane University as well as the contributors cited.

I am governed by a deep and abiding belief in humanity. My parents, Laura Bax and Donald Decuir instilled that in my siblings and me. Though sometimes it appears that the opposite is true, evil will never conquer good. My mother taught me to listen to music with a third ear. I learned to listen carefully and discover that there is always something deeper to the melodies, lyrics, artists, etc. It is because of her and unlike most of my classmates, I was familiar with Sarah Vaughn, Billie Holiday, Stan Getz, T-Bone Walker, and others by the time I entered the fourth grade. Much of my inspiration comes from the greatest sisters anyone could ask for. Veronica, Katherine, Anna (who created this book cover), Claudine, and Karen are all extremely talented and intellectual. They have given me equally talented and intellectual nieces and nephews, who are doing great things in this world, and I love them all. My brother David is the greatest musician I know. My wife Lynn has always been there and picks me up whenever I fall. My grandchildren fill my heart with joy, and our newest, Aria will be here in weeks. Beyond contributing to the scholarship about Louis Armstrong and the period considered here, I wanted to leave something for them and our posterity. If silly Paw-Paw can do this, you can too.

I am blessed to have four beautiful children, Nakiya, Jamar, David and Ebony who I love very much and dedicate this book to.

CHAPTER 1

ARMSTRONG'S AND THE PERIOD'S ORIGINS

When questioned about the possible relationship or cross influences between Harlem Renaissance writers, artists, and musicians, a college professor said that any interactions and consequential inspirational art was minimal at best. He surmised that the Harlem Renaissance writers were merely imitating French impressionists, and the canon they produced was subpar.[2] This research challenges that point of view through exploration of the influence of one of the period's seminal performing artists, Louis Armstrong. To this end, this research will show the interrelationships and cross influences of the period's literary, visual, and performing artists as well as the prevailing political and philosophical thoughts.

Armstrong's improvisational choices helped ignite a variety of artistic activities during the period known as the Harlem Renaissance. In addition to the interrelatedness of Louis Armstrong's creative decisions and the period's literary and visual arts, this research examines the impact of Armstrong's art and blues music on the political and philosophical debate during the Harlem Renaissance. A successful exploration into Armstrong's and subsequently the period's art, political, and philosophical entities requires one to examine the sources of the

---

[2] This researcher was enrolled in music as a major course of study at Southern University at New Orleans, and the University of California, Berkeley.

musician's unique culture in New Orleans. The exploration will thus include the area's West African approaches to making music in Congo Square, as well as the European musical influences, and the ebb and flow of racial relations that affected Armstrong's life and choices. The reader will note such activity in Figure 1.

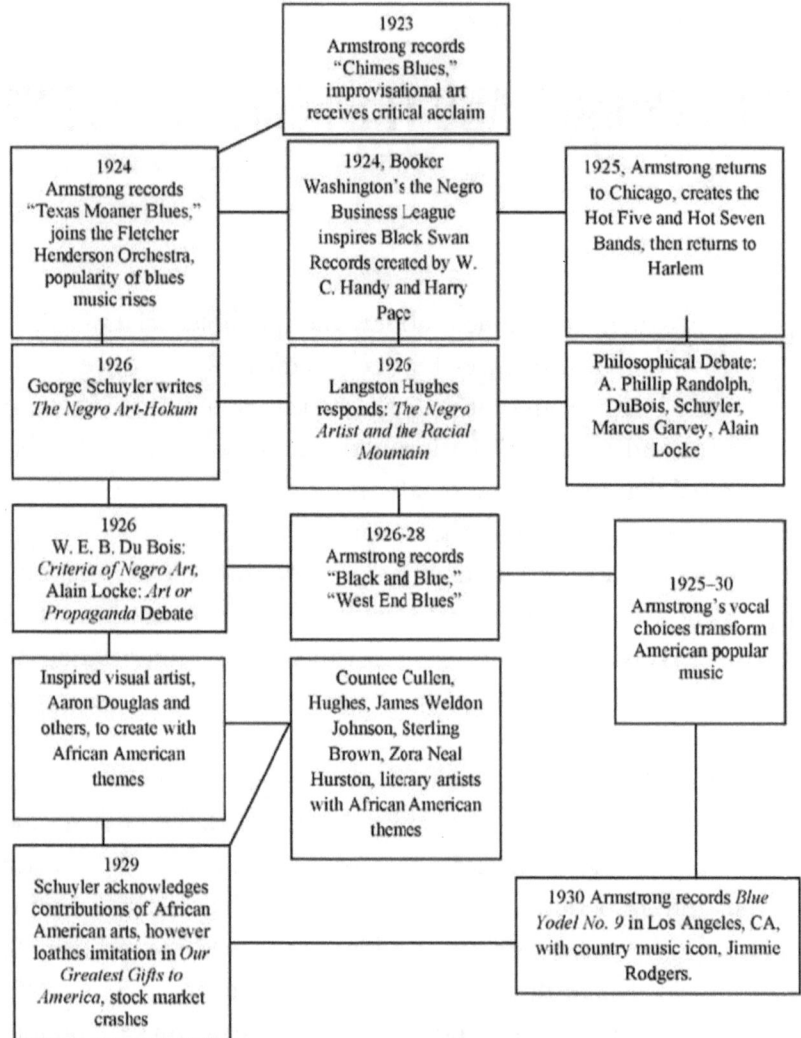

Figure 1. Louis Armstrong's artistic contributions and interrelated artistic, political, and philosophical events, 1923–1930

Armstrong's improvisational art, particularly his approach to blues music, was a significant contributor to the rise in the art's popularity. Indeed, the performing art served as the subject or inspiration for much of the period's literary and visual arts. Artistic contributions, though in various mediums, were interrelated and shared cross-influences. Not unlike other cultural or artistic eras, the Harlem Renaissance artists were aware of each other's works. In various mediums, visual artists Aaron Douglas and Archibald Motley (among others) used blues music, and the ambiance created in some of the performing art's Harlem venues as its themes. Subsequent chapters in this research will explore the use of blues music as the subject of poetic creations of some of the period's important literary artists. They include, among others, Langston Hughes, Sterling Brown, and James Weldon Johnson. Philosophically, George Schuyler, W. E. B. Du Bois, and Alain Locke contributed to the debate as to the existence, purpose, and quality of the period's arts. These cultural matters were simultaneous with Louis Armstrong's contributions to the period. Specifically, his initial foray with Joe "King" Oliver on "Chimes Blues," collaboration with Bessie Smith on W.C. Handy's composition "St. Louis Blues," recordings of "Black and Blue," and the seminal "West End Blues."

Armstrong and the period's art were not coincidental, unrelated events, but an evolvement of creativity spurred by the desire to express pride in the historical and cultural contributions of Africa and African Americans to this country and the world. The former is evidenced in the admonitions of artistic works such as Carter G. Woodson's *The Mis-Education of the Negro*, Langston Hughes's *I Too Am America*, a short-lived but important publication by a collection of seminal literary artists titled *Fire*, and Alain Locke's *The New Negro* among others. Armstrong's improvisational art, particularly his approach to blues music, was a major contributor to the rise in the art's popularity. The performing art served as an aquifer to much of the period's literary and visual art. Artistic contributions, though in various mediums, were interrelated.

Contrary to the opinion of the professor, the literary art of Langston Hughes, Countee Cullen, and Zora Neal Hurston, among others, were not celebrated in the context of French imitators but were indicative of the creative energy present in Harlem during the third decade of the twentieth century. In separate camps, visual and performing artists too contributed to the period's art.[3] The genius was in their ability to speak to the soul and essence of the African American experience.

Early West African Cultural Influences in New Orleans and Subsequently on Louis Armstrong's and the Period's Arts

The growing popularity of jazz and blues music during the third decade of the twentieth century, as well as the emergence of the period known as the Harlem Renaissance, did not take place in a cultural vacuum. The visual, performing, and literary arts produced during the period embraced African American mores and folkways. Therefore, it is necessary to explore Louis Armstrong's contributions to the period in a historical context. This research explores some of the vestiges of West African history that influenced the music and cultural behaviors of the New Orleans enslaved population. One discovers (when placed in a historical context) that Armstrong's art is partly a result of the performing arts' practices during the decades before and after the Civil War. They include vestiges of West African music in an area called Congo Square and its subsequent influence on the cultural behaviors of the city's people of color. European performing arts genres were equally influential as the city (during the nineteenth century) was home to two opera houses, while formal balls were prevalent, often employing Black musicians. Their employment was testimony to a musical versatility necessary to satisfy employers whose refined palates were nurtured by life in arguably America's most musical city. Indeed, the documented behaviors and resulting rituals cultivated a cultural uniqueness that

---

[3] David Levering Lewis's *The Portable Harlem Renaissance Reader* is an excellent resource in this regard.

influenced the city's early jazz pioneers and, subsequently, Louis Armstrong.[4]

Though the enslaved that congregated in Congo Square may have been generations removed from their ancestors' native land, evidence shows that they made every effort to recall the cultural significance and purpose in their weekly gatherings. More importantly, and pertinent to the Harlem Renaissance, documentation exits of West African historical and cultural contributions to world civilization. The contributions manifested themselves in the customs and cultural behaviors practiced by the enslaved and their posterity. Therefore, it is necessary to conduct a careful (though brief, as attention to the broader subject demands such) exploration of the West African sources and how the New Orleans artistic diaspora shared it with the world, to fully comprehend the roots of the Harlem Renaissance's performing arts.

---

[4] Congo Square is an area in New Orleans where the enslaved Africans gathered weekly on Sundays Witnesses documented the West African cultural behaviors, particularly the music-making proclivities.

ETHNIC GROUPS IN WEST AFRICA DURING THE SLAVE TRADE

African historians Cheikh Ante Diop, Al Bakri, and Ivan Van Sertima, in various research publications, detailed the cultural and political atmosphere in West Africa. Notably, the authors examined and published historical data about the peoples of Mali, Songhay, and Ghanaian empires from the tenth to nineteenth centuries.[5] Diop especially noted the pre- and post-Islamic influences on West African culture, particularly music, which had a significant bearing on the music heard in Congo Square. The cultural lineage from West Africa to the enslaved diaspora in Congo Square becomes clear after careful

---

[5] Ivan Van Sertima's *They Came Before Columbus: The African Presence in America* (New York: Random House 1976), 110–24.

exploration. Significantly, twelve of the first thirteen slave ships that arrived in Louisiana came from the Senegambia region in West Africa. France endorsed the enterprise under the auspices of the Company of the Indies. To this end, the earliest enslaved Africans brought to Louisiana in 1719 and 1743 were Senegambians, Mande, and Wolof from the Upper Guinea region, and from Ouidah. From the Lower Guinea region, the Ndongo and Kongo peoples were too enslaved and brought to Louisiana.[6] The diverse groups brought with them diverse languages, customs, mores, and traditions of music making. In separate but intertwined histories, the groups were a part of West African history of civilization rich in contributions to Western history and culture. Additionally, the West Africans' belief systems were also as diverse. Many, such as the enslaved Bambara, maintained their own ancient ancestral-worship concept. Indeed, their belief systems were centuries older than the relatively new European Christian-based faiths. The introduction of these relatively new faiths to the continent was primarily a part of a grand scheme to monopolize the lucrative slave trade in the western hemisphere, and later dominate the excavation of the vast raw materials present on the continent. Still, other Africans embraced the relatively new concept of Islam. Musically, each had distinct practices, be it the stratified-percussive-rhythmic-based music of the non-Islamic faiths or the melismatic chants present in early Catholic worship practices, or the Muslim prayer worship. It is possible that, in many cases, the early music of the enslaved may have evolved into a hybrid of it all.

To this end, the largest ethnic enslaved population during the early years in Louisiana were the Senegambians. Although Senegambia's role in the slave trade diminished, their cultural significance remained. According to researcher Gwendolyn Midlo-Hall, "Senegambia remained an important source of the slaves brought to Louisiana throughout the

---

[6] See Diop's publication, *Pre-Colonial Black Africa* (Chicago: Lawrence Hill Books, 1987); Al Bakri, "The Book of Routes and Realms," in *Corpus of Early Arabic Sources for West Africa* (New York: Ned Sublette, *The World That Made New Orleans: From Spanish Silver to Congo Square* (Chicago: Lawrence Hill Books, 2009), 60.

eighteenth century."⁷ Historically, the Senegambians' ancestral land was home to medieval civilizations, Ghana and Mali. Significantly, the Louisiana Senegambians were descendants of a people whose contributions to African history are centuries old. Geographically, they lived in an area from the Atlantic Ocean east to the Nile River. The Senegambians were both contributors and benefactors of a geographic region that flourished for centuries, fermenting an exchange of goods and philosophies. Their ancestors contributed to the creation of the historically significant cities of Jenne, Gao, and Timbuktu, and the group's centuries-old trade routes allowed for interaction with the city-states present in Songhay and Mali during the Common Era. According to New Orleans historian Ned Sublette, "One would suppose that the music of the Africans in Louisiana during the French period bore a strong resemblance to the music of the Senegambians, the homeland of the majority of its people."⁸ It is of significant note here that the early enslaved population brought to Louisiana a degree of the humanities (performing and visual arts), which was part of their homeland experience. Historian Patrick Manning discussed an African propensity to exchange cultural ideas: "Yet another way to trace travel and communication across African lands is to follow the movement of material culture from one region to another."⁹ The movement of material culture, including music-making practices, is salient to the theoretical proposition that the mores and folkways Louis Armstrong experienced in New Orleans were West African. Specifically, the city's area, known as Congo Square, was one of the few places where the enslaved Africans practiced cultural behaviors, including music and dance, without limits placed upon them by their captors. Their contributions became essential to what was to become the relatively unique New Orleans culture. Equally important were the cultural influences of the many divergent

---

[7] Gwendolyn Midlo Hall, *Africans in Colonial Louisiana: The Development of Afro-Creole Culture in the Eighteenth Century* (Baton Rouge: Louisiana State University Press, 1992) 31.

[8] Ibid., 60.

[9] Patrick Manning, *The African Diaspora: A History Through Culture* (New York: Columbia University Press, 2010), 40.

people of European descent living in the city. Researcher Greer Mendy commented on the historical importance of Black dance on the region's history and culture: "Black dance traditions in Louisiana began as early as the arrival of Africans in the new Louisiana territory. They have continued to transform into new expressions through the evolution of Louisiana's Black culture."[10]

The importance of stringed instruments in the Senegambian culture and their importation to the performance practices in Congo Square is evident in the drawings rendered by Benjamin Latrobe, a frequent visitor to the Sunday gatherings. The string instrument Latrobe sketched has the appearance of an indigenous Senegambian instrument called a *kora*. Indeed, the West African region considered here also was home to a tradition of bowed string instruments. According to Sublette, "Fiddles came to French Louisiana from two directions: from Europe, but also from Africa, because the Senegambians had a bowed-instrument tradition, and had possibly had it as long as, or longer than France. In the New World, the Senegambians' musical knowledge could be expressed on the European violin, as well as on the banjo, an instrument that derives from a Senegambian family of plucked instruments."[11]

Despite the banning of weekly gatherings at Congo Square, the performance practices of the enslaved continued to be an essential part of the city's culture. City leaders relaxed the ban on Congo Square gatherings circa 1845, and the weekly cultural activities resumed. By that time, many such as violinist Massa Quamba, banjo player William Martin, and a revered vocalist Signor Cornmeali earned reputations as outstanding musicians. The musicians were integral to a municipality that seemed to have endless parties, balls, and dances, juxtaposed with two flourishing opera houses. Visitors described New Orleans during the years preceding and after the Civil War as a city with a propensity for dancing. It is of significant note that by then, the performing art on display by the enslaved often consisted of European folk melodies. Henry

---

[10] Greer E. Mendy, *Black Dance in Louisiana, Guardian of a Culture* (New Orleans: Tekrema Center for African Diaspora Cultural Literacy, 2017) 11.
[11] Ibid., 60.

Kmen opines, "Moreover, observers tell of seeing jigs, fandangos, and Virginia breakdowns in the square, and they speak of hearing melodies like 'Old Virginia Never Tire,' 'Hey Jim Along Josey,' and 'Get Along You Yellow Gals.' However, much of the primitive music played there was in the Congo Square dances; it seemed apparent that they were borrowing rapidly from the culture around them."[12] The melting pot that was New Orleans in the city's early years was integral to the culture that produced jazz. In *Swing That Music*, Armstrong opined on the origins of jazz music: "It came up slowly out of the old negro folk songs and the spirituals, and the regular beat of jazz syncopation probably came out of the strumming of the banjoes which the slaves had learned to play after the Civil War. Some say it went to the tom-toms of our people in Africa before we were civilized. And it might be."[13] Armstrong obviously was not aware of the true history of his African ancestry.

Arguably, no other area in the United States had a more concentrated, diverse population than Louis Armstrong's place of birth, New Orleans. Researcher Rick Coleman offered this opinion: "With a true melting pot of French, African, Native American, German, Spanish, and Caribbean inhabitants, New Orleans became the heart that pumped a very different cultural message upstream against the overwhelming white-Anglo-Saxon-Protestant current in America."[14] To this end, Louis Armstrong came of age in an area inundated with what may have been America's most diverse cultural region and West Africa was a chief contributor to that culture. Hence, the sources of Armstrong's art (rhythmic differentiation and improvisation) and much of the region's mores are cultural recollections of West African musical practices and windows to the folkways of his ancestral homeland. The task afoot is to show the connection between his and the period's art and the

---

[12] Henry Kmen, *Music in New Orleans: The Formative Years, 1791–1841* (Baton Rouge: Louisiana State University Press, 1966), 229.
[13] Louis Armstrong, *Swing That Music* (New York, Da Capo Press Centennial Edition, 1993) 9.
[14] Rick Coleman, *Blue Monday: Fats Domino and the Lost Dawn of Rock N' Roll* (New York: Da Capo Press 2006), 1.

enslaved collective African musical recollections in Congo Square and, subsequently, America.

The area's cultural uniqueness is a product of (though not exclusively) cultural interactions between the enslaved Africans, Europeans, and the region's aboriginal people. By the third decade of the nineteenth century and up to the Civil War, the African slave trade expanded. In addition to the African groups listed earlier, the population in south-eastern Louisiana also included Angolans, Congolese, Bambarans, Akans, Ibos, Ewe, and Yorubans and/or their recent descendants. They interacted with area's European peoples, which included French, English, Spanish, Italians, Germans, and European-Americans (most of whom were non-slaveholders). There was also a significant presence of free people of color, and the native population, which included Choctaw, Biloxi, and Creek nations, among others. Pertinent to this research is the perspective of foreign travelers to New Orleans and West Africa, which reveals similarities in the approach to music making. They included the use of encircled drums in ritual fashion as well as the use of timbre in the context of polyrhythms. Benjamin Latrobe[15] and British explorer Mongo Park[16] on separate occasions noted not only the hospitality they experienced as visitors, but also the intricacies and interactions between the musicians, dancers, and pertinent stakeholders. Latrobe's experience came while visiting Congo Square in New Orleans. Park's encounter with the culture came while visiting West Africa.

The creators of the music that subsequently influenced Armstrong's artistic choices during the Harlem Renaissance mirrored the folkways and customs of the enslaved Africans in Congo Square. Their musical approach, particularly the recognition of the timbral importance of the instruments and vocals, is intertwined with the enslaves' stratified creations. In the context of the Congo Square and West African performing art, the musicians too were expected to embrace individuality

---

[15] Benjamin Latrobe, *The Journal of Latrobe: Being the Notes and Sketches of an Architect, Naturalist and Traveler in the United States from 1796 to 1820* (New York: Burt Franklin, 1971), 175-81.

[16] Mongo Park, *The Journal of a Mission to the Interior of Africa in the Year 1805* (London: John Murray, 1815), 200–202; 275–76; 319–21.

and timbral considerations while staying in the context of the music-making task at hand. Indeed, early jazz blossomed from the necessity of establishing roles in the performing arts context. Specifically, traditional wind instruments in early New Orleans jazz groups each established a melody, countermelody, and underlying chordal movement. Usually, the roles were initially distributed (per song) between trumpet or cornet, clarinet, and trombone, respectively. The artists alternately played and/or improvised the melody, often using a degree of ornamentation while maintaining an underlying prescribed chordal progression.[17] Thus began the development of specific musical functions or roles necessary to ensure the success of any particular performance. Indeed, consideration of musical roles, and detailed attention paid to instrumental and voice timbre, were imitative of the West African approach to music-making and integral to the development of jazz music.

Consequently, two decades after the Civil War, the descendants of the Congo Square musicians began playing European wind instruments establishing the distinct New Orleans polyphony with their ancestral West African musical sensibilities. Indeed, many second-generation blues and jazz musicians such as Louis Armstrong, Sidney Bechet, and Joe "King" Oliver carried out those sensibilities throughout the Harlem Renaissance and beyond. The weekly cultural gatherings of the enslaved described earlier by Benjamin Latrobe gave rise to musical practices that were precursors to the creation of early jazz music.[18] There are no recordings of the music performed in Congo Square. However, one can analyze contemporary performances of West African percussion folk music and get a glimpse of their ancestral music from two and a half centuries earlier. The Congo Square musicians performed rhythmic patterns on make-shift drums as the enslaved danced, sang, and collectively recalled the mores and folkways of their West African ancestral homeland. Amiri Baraka suggested that "West Africans had specific musical sensibilities regarding rhythm: the reason for the remarkable development of the

---

[17] See the musical transcription of *Texas Moaner Blues,* Figure 2, page 35.
[18] See Sidney Bechet's description of his enslaved grandfather (a musician at Congo Square) in his autobiography *Treat It Gentle* (Cambridge: DaCapo Press, 1958), 45–61.

rhythmic qualities of African music can certainly be traced to the fact that Africans also used the drums for communication and not, as once thought, merely in a kind of primitive Morse code, but by the phonetic reproduction of the words themselves—the result being that Africans developed an extremely complex rhythmic sense, as well as becoming unusually responsive to timbral subtleties."[19]

According to Latrobe, several enslaved Africans were playing makeshift percussion instruments, while others were dancing:

> They were formed into circular groups, in the midst of four of which that I examined (but there were more of them) was a ring, the largest not ten feet in diameter. In the first were two women dancing. They held each a coarse handkerchief, extended by the corners in their hands, and set to each other in a miserably dull and slow figure, hardly moving their feet or bodies. The music consisted of two drums and a stringed instrument. An old man set astride of a cylindrical drum, about a foot in diameter, and beat it with incredible quickness with the edge of his hands and fingers. The other drum was an opened staved thing held between the knees and beaten the same way.[20]

Latrobe further stated, "The most curious instrument, however no doubt was a stringed instrument, which was imported from Africa."[21] Latrobe notes an elderly gentleman singing, "A man sang an uncouth song to the dancing, and the women screamed a detestable burden on one single note. The allowed amusements of Sunday have, it seems, perpetuated here those of Africa among its former inhabitants…"[22] Latrobe's last point reveals the difficulty in assigning Western-art music criticism to non-Western music.

---

[19] Ibid., 26.
[20] Benjamin Latrobe, *Journal of Latrobe* (New York: D. Appleton, 1905), 179–81.
[21] Ibid., 180.
[22] Ibid.

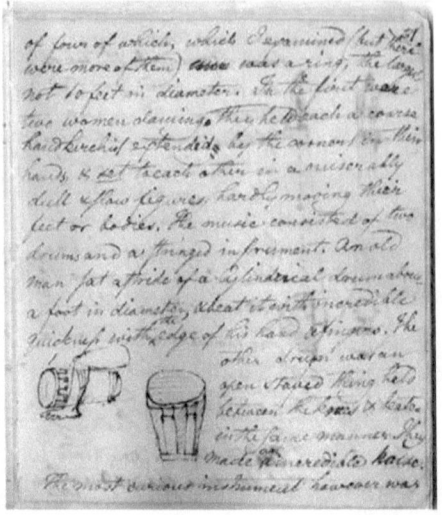

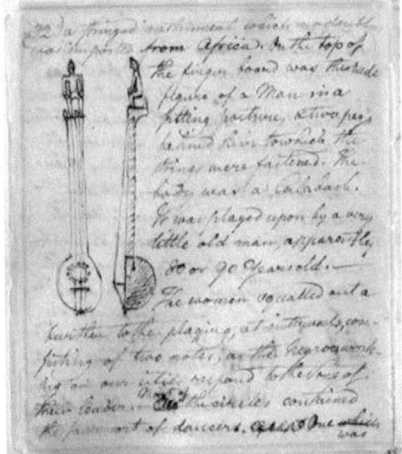 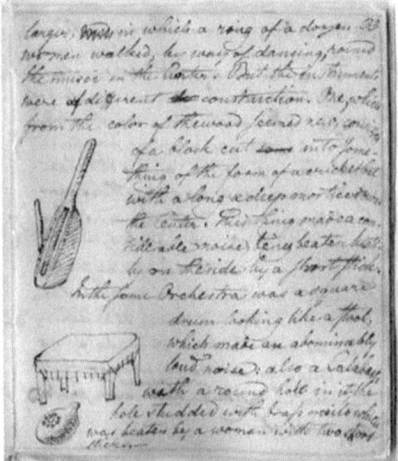

Latrobe's Drawings (Congo Square) Latrobe's Drawings (Congo Square) (Maryland Center for History & Culture)

Theoretically, the creation of blues and jazz music did not happen in a cultural vacuum. The performing art was not supervening to cultural behaviors and musical approach present in Congo Square. The early blues music creators, just as the enslaved musicians of Congo Square, were not making music because they were happy or satisfied with their social status. Conversely, the desire to make themselves happy or gain a melancholy relief was an inspiration for the music making. This writer explores this theory in greater detail and in the context of creating blues music in Chapter Four. Decades later and in reaction to post-antebellum life in the region, the descendants of the enslaved performing artists in Congo Square used the same music approach and rationale. Specifically they invented a cultural and artistic reaction as not only a coping mechanism, but a conscience protest to the laws (Black Codes) enacted to eliminate the freedoms gained during Reconstruction. Deeper still, this researcher believes that the late nineteenth-century blues and jazz-music pioneers were exhibiting cultural recollections of their enslaved foreparents.

Among the similarities between West African and African American music discovered by composer and musicologist Olly Wilson were such practices as percussive body usage, communal approach to music making, call response, the creation of a heterogeneous sound ideal, and poly or stratified rhythms. Wilson researched the music and cultural behaviors in Ghana and published his findings. His theories are of vital importance in the context of the practice of call and response in a solo performing art setting. According to Wilson, "This partially is a result of the stratification commonly found in the instrumental music of the culture area we are considering, but it is also present in solo songs—where the singer seems to furnish his own counter voice."[23] Interestingly, Latrobe's description describes all of the musical practices described by Wilson. If one assumes as did Sublette that the music heard in Congo Square was Senegambian (West African), then musicians played percussion instruments with various timbres. Subsequently, each instrument had a specific role depending on the song of choice. Indeed, the cultural behavior of communal music making in which nonmusicians or spectators participate still exists today not only in the New Orleans region but also in African American and American popular musical traditions. Not unlike the music of the enslaved in other regions, the music produced in Congo Square served different functions. It often provided a melancholy relief to the performing artists and stakeholders as well as welcomed recollections of

---

[23] Olly Wilson, "The Significance of the Relationship between Afro-American Music and West African Music," *Black Perspectives in Music* 2, no.1 (Spring 1974): 16.

their ancestral homeland. Music Professor Malesha Taylor described the cultural behavior as acts of sonic resistance, and a return to Africanism through performing art expressions.[24] The fervor and desire for freedom continued through the Civil War years and beyond. Not unlike other municipalities in the South, New Orleans struggled with the hypocrisy of building an economy on slave labor.

Contrary to a persistent but inaccurate narrative of American history, resistance to enslavement and the quest for freedom was ever-present. The enslaved were far from docile people with a propensity to create music. Activity in Congo Square was reduced significantly circa 1817 when city leaders elected to restrict such gatherings, possibly because of an unsuccessful slave uprising. They feared that such reprisals were the manifestations of a quest for liberty pervasive during the post-American and French Revolutions as well as the quests for freedom among the enslaved populations in the Caribbean colonies. Specifically, in 1795, a group of enslaved Africans on planter John Poydras's sugar plantation in Point Coupee parish devised a plan to earn freedom, which included killing Poydras. The failed revolt followed an earlier thwarted uprising in nearby Bayou Lafourche. The historical ramifications on Louisiana's and New Orleans's legacy of racial discrimination, which impacted Armstrong's early life, is significant. Historian Gwendolyn Midlo Hall opines, "Historical myths about the Point Coupee Conspiracy of 1795 were deeply implanted into the consciousness of white Louisianans. They became the cornerstone justifying racist violence and oppression of Afro-Louisianians and of whites who opposed slavery and racism."[25] Indeed, the enslaved performing in Congo Square and those living in the surrounding plantations were aware of the desires for individual liberty present in the American and French Revolutions. They were also aware of the successes of the slave revolt in Haiti. Despite the failure of the Point Coupee plans, they continued to internalize and acted upon an ever-present desire for freedom. The uprising was indeed carefully planned though the result was continued bondage.

---

[24] "Malesha Taylor, Discussion at The Institute of Black Intellectual Innovation Conference, "Innovating Sound: Sonic Resistance and Ray Charles." April 20, 2021.
[25] Ibid., 344.

Indeed, the slave revolt of 1811 was militaristic, and it undoubtedly influenced the ruling class and city leaders' actions. The freedom fighters recalled the logistics of their native African tribal conflicts and donned the military uniforms taken from the slaveholders during the quest for liberty. Among the leaders of the uprising were veterans of recent West African civil unrest. Researcher Daniel Rasmussen discussed three specific revolutionaries and the use of music for communication and inspiration. Specifically, the revolt's organizer, Charles Deslondes, and two veterans of recent tribal wars, Kook and Quamana. According to Rasmussen: "With the addition of Kook and Quamana's detachment of Akan warriors, the slave army now numbered well over one hundred men. Beating drums and shouting with the joy of freedom, they urged each other on."[26] Ironically, one year later, during the War of 1812, General Andrew Jackson's army included enslaved Africans, free men of color, French, German, Spanish settlers as well as Native Americans, all indicative of the city's population during the formative years of jazz and blues music.[27]

Possibly, more than any other community in the United States, the area had to come to grips with the legacy of "free men of color" juxtaposed with the enslaved population and how the interrelationships between the groups manifested musically during the dawning of new American music, ragtime, blues, and jazz. Such was the music tradition Louis Armstrong learned as a child and executed as an adolescent in New Orleans. The musical and genealogical lineage is confirmed when the reader discovers the life and death of an enslaved musician named Omar, the maternal grandfather of early jazz pioneer Sidney Bechet, and a practicing musician in Congo Square. Omar's legacy more than likely took place during the years when cultural activities revamped after circa 1845. Bechet discussed Omar's saga, including the desperate attempt of Omar to maintain a love affair with another slave who carried his child and was under the control of another area slaveholder. Bechet proudly

---

[26] David Rasmussen, *American Uprising: The Untold Story of America's Largest Slave Revolt* (New York: Harper Perennial, 2011) 107.

[27] See Henry Kmen's *Music in New Orleans* (Baton Rouge: Louisiana State University Press), vii, viii.

described his grandfather and his African heritage in his autobiography: "It's all true, all that was said about my grandfather. And it's all so mixed up with the music. In Paris it's like I can hear all that was happening to it when my grandfather was making (music) it, back in those days when it had just been brought from Africa and was still finding itself in the South."[28] Bechet also explained the poignant reason for his adopted country: "I knew why, France it's closer to Africa. I've wanted to be as close to it as I could. It's the mood, you'd call it, an atmosphere I wanted to put myself into. My grandfather, he was Africa."[29]

Significantly, the performing art present in Congo Square was an influence on one of America's first virtuoso musicians and composers in the Western or European tradition. Native New Orleanian, Louis Moreau Gottschalk lived near Congo Square and heard the music of the enslaved. In 1848, he composed a piano piece based upon his recollections of the music he heard. Interestingly, the piece, written when Gottschalk was recovering from an illness in France, is evidence of the enslaves' polyphonic and polyrhythmic approach to making music. The same approach adopted by early New Orleans jazz creators. Gottschalk had a moment of serendipity when he revisited the composition after successful convalescence. Biographer Vernon Loggins opined,

> Soon it dawned upon him that what he had taken to be three unrelated themes were in reality well integrated and that he held in his hands the sketch for a composition in all respects a unit. It was music such that he never played, but it seemed to him to possess power and charm. When he tried it out on piano, he liked it still more. There could, he decided, be only one title for the piece.
>
> —"Bamboula: Danse des Negres."[30]

---

[28] Ibid., 79.
[29] Bechet, *Treat It Gentle,* 79.
[30] Vernon Loggins, *Where the World Ends* (Baton Rouge: Louisiana State University Press, 1958), 72.

Sublette considered the source of Gottschalk's composition in a set of questions: "Was Gottschalk, a programmatic composer, drawing a sound portrait of a dance at Congo Square? And might he be inadvertently telling us that the singing, drumming, and dancing circles put popular melodies into their own rhythm and style? That is to say, were they doing what jazz musicians were doing fifty years later?"[31]

The years following the Civil War and Reconstruction and the advent of the Black Codes witnessed an attempted nullification of the Thirteenth, Fourteenth, and Fifteenth Amendments.[32] The effect of the Black Codes proved to be devastating and an aquifer for an African American aesthetic associated with the quest for access to constitutionally guaranteed liberty. More significantly was the reaction or conscience rebellion by the former enslaved and the second and third generations of post-Civil War musicians to the relatively neo-oppressive atmosphere. They chose to continue the cultural behaviors and musical practices of their enslaved foreparents and African ancestors. Simultaneously, there was an influx of formerly enslaved groups who migrated to New Orleans from the interior of Mississippi and elsewhere who, in turn, introduced a type of music born out of spirituals, field hollers, and work songs. The relatively new performing art was called the "blues." Subsequently, circa 1890, early New Orleans African American musicians such as Buddy Bolden, Freddy Keppard, and Sidney Bechet began playing a hybrid of ragtime, blues, and spirituals with the musical approach (specific roles, timbre considerations, and improvisational choices) passed down from Congo Square. They played this new genre in performing arts ensembles using different European wind and percussion instruments that had been prevalent in the region's Western music tradition most of the nineteenth century. Researcher Samuel Floyd Jr. argued,

---

[31] Ned Sublette, *The World That Made New Orleans Famous: From Spanish Silver to Congo Square*, 125.

[32] Historically, the reactionary violent behavior to end Reconstruction in Louisiana came in 1880 at the battle of Canal Street when terrorist groups murdered hundreds of Blacks and forced many out of the city. Coincidently, Louisiana's first Black governor, P. B. S. Pinchback, is the grandfather of Harlem Renaissance writer Jean Toomer.

> The banjo, flute triangle, drum, quills, and sticks (bones) were ubiquitous in slave culture. It is not surprising to find that this combination of instruments is perfectly suited to the realization of the heterogeneous sound ideal. The combination of these sounds creates a contrasting, not a blending, conglomerate, resulting in a sound that is ideally suited to the rhythmic, polyphonic, and tonal stratifications of African and African-American music.[33]

What Latrobe and others contemporaneously heard were performing arts that were simultaneously historical recollections of collective cultural behaviors and primitive arts. Blues music historian Albert Murray discussed the difference between folk art and primitive art. In the context of the developing performing art, the early New Orleans jazz-music pioneers codified an indigenous American art form. "Primitive arts and crafts are sophisticated. They are not the crude imitation, corruption, vulgarization, or popularization of a more sophisticated stylization. They represent the very highest refinement of rituals and technologies of a given culture."[34]

The manifestation of a "communal" approach to making music identified by Olly Wilson is present in many of the region's customs, mores, and behaviors, particularly in the African American community.[35] Succinctly, West African and African American musicians considered it a positive affirmation when nonmusicians joined the performance art. Consumers became participants by singing along, dancing, using parts of their bodies, or any objects percussively. Jazz historians Donald D. Megill and Richard S. Demory agreed: "Everyone within earshot was expected to participate. There were few passive observers. A typical performance would have a leader, accompanied by drummers and possible other instrumentalists, who called out rhythmic words or

---

[33] Samuel Floyd Jr., *The Power of Black Music* (New York: Oxford University Press, 1995), 56.
[34] Albert Murray, *Stomping the Blues* (New York: Da Capo Press, 1976) 208.
[35] Ibid., 15.

phrases. The participating 'audience,' clapping in time and moving in unison, would shout a response."[36] The authors surmised further: "African music making thus was a collective experience in which everyone had the opportunity for self-transcendence through music."[37] Indeed, audience or consumer participation at a music-making event became the main staple in New Orleans culture.

The "communal" approach to making music was obvious to Armstrong, and most New Orleanians immersed in the area's folkways. Indeed, the venues for early jazz musicians and frequented by a young Armstrong included bars, dance halls, brothels, and pertinent to this discussion, parades where early brass bands flourished. Customarily, bands would play to attract an audience for an upcoming event or the initiation of an affair. In some cases, they would perform an impromptu parade or at a busy neighborhood intersection. In every instance, the communal approach to music making (in which the audience is encouraged to join in) is expected, consequently giving the musicians a sense of validation. Indeed, bands and musicians use this practice to determine their worth and success; coincidently, young Armstrong was aware of the rivalries.

Armstrong's sense of competitiveness juxtaposed with a keen awareness of his audience's satisfaction was born out of his experiences, observing the custom of musical battles. Social behavior was an integral part of the region's folkways. In his memoir *Satchmo: My Life in New Orleans*, Armstrong recalled an incident when one of his mentors, Joe "King" Oliver's band joins forces with Kid Ory's band and participated in a tradition of promoting competing events through their performance art:

> Kid Ory and Joe Oliver got together and made one of the hottest bands that ever hit New Orleans. They often played in a tail gate wagon to advertise a ball or entertainments. When they found themselves on a street corner next to another band in another wagon, Joe and

---

[36] Donald Megill and Richard S. Demory, *Introduction to Jazz History* (Englewood Cliffs: Prentice-Hall Inc., 1984), 2.

[37] Ibid., 2.

> King Oliver would shoot the works. They would give all that good mad music under their belts and the crowd would go wild. When the other band decided to cut the competition and start out for another corner, Kid Ory a little tune that made the crowd go wild again."[38]

Armstrong also recalled experiencing the same wrath from the Oliver/ Ory group:

> One day when we were advertising for a ball we ran into Oliver and his band. I was not feeling well that day and I forgot to stand up. What a licking those guys gave us. Sure enough when our wagon started to leave, Kid Ory started to play that get-away tune at us. The crowd went mad. We felt terrible about it but we took it like good sports there was not any other band that could do that to us. We youngsters were the closest rivals the Ory band had.[39]

Musicians challenging each other to establish a hierarchy while promoting cultural events were commonplace in New Orleans. Armstrong's recollections here are but one example of many folkways that made the area, though not exclusive, unique.

The rituals associated with funerals in New Orleans also have vestiges of West African performing arts and cultural behaviors. Before the burial of the deceased, mourners commonly display melancholy behavior. The corresponding ceremony does not necessarily take place in a church but sometimes in someone's home or funeral parlor. In some cases, such organizations as social and pleasure clubs, which initially were mutual aid societies, stepped in to assist with the financial burden inherited by the family of the deceased. Mourners danced in the streets in celebration of the deceased's memory. This cultural behavior remains today. Often,

---

[38] Louis Armstrong, *Satchmo: My Life In New Orleans* (N0ew York, Da Capo Press, 1954) 97–8.
[39] Ibid., 98.

mourners migrate to the deceased's home or some prearranged place after the burial to console the bereaved family. Usually, a traditional brass band wind instruments (conducive for outside performances, which include a sousaphone) leads the dancers (moaners) through the neighborhood. Armstrong commented on the uniqueness of the event: "The funerals in New Orleans are sad until the body is finally lowered into the grave and the reverend says 'ashes to ashes and dust to dust.' After the brother was six feet underground [sic], the band would strike up one of those good old tunes like *Didn't He Ramble,* and all the people would leave their worries behind."[40] Armstrong's recollections here as a participant inside the culture affirm the dual purpose of the music. It functions as a conduit for the rituals associated with burials in the region as well as a tool for melancholy relief.

The region's cultural behaviors mirror West African communities, including the Ewe, Akhan, and Ibo peoples who have a similar belief system and customs regarding funeral ceremonies. Their concept and customs with regards to funeral rituals are such that it is a celebration of the deceased life. West African scholar Malidoma Patrice Somé explains the emotional ties between the deceased, bereaved, and community in West African culture: "A community is held together by emotional ties that result in a conscience feeling of connection…"[41] Just as their African American counterparts, these West African communities give gifts of food to the family to demonstrate their sympathy and their willingness to help with the expected arrival of mourners. Musically, this cultural behavior mirrors the practices that transpired decades earlier in Congo Square. Specifically, there is an expectation that nonmusicians, spectators, and/or mourners will dance, sing, and use percussive body sounds, thus making it a communal music-making event. Samuel Floyd Jr. expressed his theory regarding the West African cultural behavior and its practices in New Orleans as follows: "The activities that took place, and still do, in the Akan dancing ring—as they did in those other

---

[40] Ibid., 91.
[41] Malidoma Patrice Somé, *The Healing Wisdom of Africa: Finding Life Purpose, Though Nature, Ritual, and Community* (New York: Jeremy P. Tarcher/Putnam, 1998) 53.

African societies— have implications for the origin of the 'second line' of New Orleans jazz funerals, for the origin and nature scat singing in early and later jazz, and for the nature of 'shouting' in African American ring ritual and its derivatives."[42] Floyd Jr.'s discussion reinforces the theory that the nuances (communal music-making, stratified rhythms, percussive body usage) of Armstrong's and the period's performing arts are West African in origin. Equally significant is the impact of Armstrong's early education, which included apprenticeships with some of jazz music's early pioneers who were successfully codifying the Africanisms and on the cusp of sharing the performing art with the residents of Harlem, New York, and the rest of the world. Just as significant culturally, are the rituals, customs, and folkways associated with New Orleans and their impact on young Louis Armstrong.

---

[42] Samuel Floyd Jr., *The Power of Black Music* (New York: Oxford University Press, 1995), 22.

CHAPTER II

THE PRECURSORS TO "TEXAS MOANER BLUES" AND ARMSTRONG'S EARLY YEARS

Not unlike other artists who have made significant contributions to American and world culture, Louis Armstrong owes much to his early education, both formal and informal, as a music apprentice in a city that embraced the exploration of ragtime, blues, and the improvisational possibilities that is jazz music. New Orleans musicians who were descendants of the enslaved lived and/or participated in a set of folkways and cultural behaviors that solidified the music-making practices brought to the region from West Africa and present in Congo Square. Not unlike other geographical regions, there was a market for the music of one's recent ancestral region. The West African music-making influence was juxtaposed with the German, French, and Italian operas. The combination was seminal to the region's performing arts. The fact that the early progenitors of the genre (some of whom were formerly enslaved) often earned a living by playing European folk songs brought to the region by recent immigrants was pertinent to the emergence of jazz music. They often could be heard playing schottisches, mazurkas, and renditions of opera excerpts. The importance here is that musically and culturally, there was an amalgamation of performing arts resulting from a diverse society. Equally important to Louis Armstrong's musical and social growth was the choice of education that confronted black leaders. Significantly, the formerly enslaved and their descendants benefit from an education that is based upon industrial training or a curriculum that teaches the sciences, humanities, and language arts?

Significantly, Armstrong and most Black youth in the South were impacted by the decision of whether to adopt an industrial or liberal arts education. The mode of education for the descendants of the enslaved inspired a robust debate before and after the period considered here. The industrial, or Hampton-Tuskegee industrial education model, emphasized training in agricultural and mechanical technology, carpentry, and domestic maintenance. Some influential black leaders aligned themselves philosophically with Booker T. Washington and believed that industrial training was the best path forward for Black Americans. His position on the established social order, particularly in the South, also inspired harsh criticism from activists. Indeed, many Southern institutions adopted the industrial education model, a fact that was integral to Armstrong's experience after his early education at Fisk School in New Orleans. His introduction to industrial education (and formal music training) came when he was criminally sentenced as a juvenile delinquent to the Colored Waif's Home for Boys.

One of Booker T. Washington's staunchest critics may have been sociologist and philosopher, W. E. B. Du Bois. He and others advocated for a liberal arts education that included a curriculum designed to prepare a student for postsecondary (relative to the time period considered here) education. Their recommended courses of study included, but not limited to, language, social studies, hard sciences, foreign language, and mathematics. Conversely, industrial education curricula included training in domestic services, agricultural studies, and mechanical aptitude. Du Bois discussed the importance of and need for an all-encompassing approach to education. "Training for life teaches living; but what training for the profitable living together of black men and white?"[43] Antilynching and social activist Ida Barnett Wells joined Du

---

[43] W. E. B. Du Bois, *The Souls of Black Folk* (New York: Barnes and Noble Books, 2003), 69.

Bois and voiced her opposition to Booker T. Washington's stance on social issues and education: "Our policy was to denounce the wrongs and injustices which were heaped upon our people, and to use whatever influences we had to help right them."[44] Wells expounded,

> Mr. Washington's theory had been that we ought not to spend our time agitating for our rights; that we had better give attention to trying to be first class people in a jim [sic] crow car than insisting that the jim crow car be abolished; that we should spend more time practicing industrial pursuits and getting education to fit us for this work than in going to college and striving for a college education.[45]

Carter G. Woodson also contributed to the discussion and opposed Eurocentric curricula that ignored the contributions of African Americans: "The education of any people should begin with the people themselves, but Negroes thus trained have been dreaming about ancients of Europe and about those who have tried to imitate them."[46] The debate over an "industrial" or "liberal arts" education (particularly during the decades preceding the Harlem Renaissance) for African Americans demonstrates more than anything the differences in the philosophies of Du Bois and Washington.

The paradigm dominated the social and political debate for much of the twentieth century. Indeed, the industrial versus liberal arts curricula, specifically in racially segregated schools, promoted a lack of confidence in the viability of historically Black colleges and universities that remains today.[47] The opposing philosophies polarized activists,

---

[44] Ida B. Wells, *Crusade for Justice: The Autobiography of Ida B. Wells* (Chicago: University of Chicago Press, 1970), 265.

[45] Ibid., 265.

[46] Carter G. Woodson, *The Mis-Education of the Negro* (Mineola, NY: Dover Publications, 1933), 21.

[47] James D. Anderson, *The Education of Blacks in the South, 1860–1935* (Chapel Hill: The University of North Carolina Press, 1988), 18–32.

philosophers, and artists. However, the decision to install a fine arts component (the school band) into the industrial education curricula is pertinent to the discussion here. Such was the case for Louis Armstrong at the Colored Waifs Home for Boys.

In New Orleans, Armstrong benefitted from an industrial education curriculum that was juxtaposed with a performing arts component, the school's band. The Colored Waifs Home for Boys was a youth detention center that also served as a temporary boarding school for juvenile delinquents. Armstrong was criminally sentenced to the institution by a juvenile-court judge after illegally discharging a firearm, and the future American music and cultural icon received his formal primary music training there. Significantly, the institution's band was an integral part of the city's culture as they participated in parades, funerals, and civic events. Of important note here is that the education of the city's wayward Black youth was in the hands of an African American war veteran. Precisely, a veteran of the Spanish-American War.

Captain Joseph Jones was named the school's headmaster, and an impressionable young Armstrong came under the influence of the military disciplinarian who also spoke Spanish and once served as a translator for President William McKinley. Coincidently, President McKinley was familiar with the Waifs Home model of industrial education, having met with Booker T. Washington and praising his work after visiting Tuskegee Institute in 1898. McKinley was particularly appreciative of Washington's acknowledgment of his (McKinley's) recognition of African American soldiers and often sought Washington's advice regarding federal appointments dedicated to Blacks.[48] One such appointment was New Orleans native, Walter L. Cohen, who served as customs inspector, and during the Theodore Roosevelt administration (Armstrong's Waifs Home years) as registrar of the US Land Office in New Orleans.

Louis Armstrong's improvisational art, and subsequently one of the principal aquifers of the Harlem Renaissance's performing, literary, and visual arts was the product of a direct correlation between the curricula, music teaching of Mr. Peter Davis, and the mentorship of Mr. and Mrs.

---

[48] Booker T. Washington, *Up from Slavery* (New York: Signet Classic 2000), 179.

Joseph Jones, the headmaster and his wife. Captain Jones's patriotism was foremost, and he insisted his staff and students have a reverence for the flag and country. According to Armstrong, "The keepers were all colored. Mr. Jones, a young man who had recently served in the cavalry, drilled us every morning in the court in front of the Waifs Home and we were taught the manual of arms with wooden guns."[49] Captain Jones's presence in Armstrong's life proved essential to his existential growth as a citizen and musician.

It is important to note that Jones's life and contributions to the education of disadvantaged youth in New Orleans were indicative of cultural critic and period naysayer George Schuyler's argument that patriotism, discipline, and artistic conformity are the virtues necessary for African American social advancement. Of equal importance to Armstrong was the impact of the institution's band director, Mr. Peter Davis. After initial trepidation (because of the reputation of Armstrong's neighborhood), Davis became one of the young musician's early supporters. He shared the experience of earning Davis's trust after weeks of playing the alto, as the band and school's new bugler. "I felt real proud of my position as bugler. I would stand very erect as I would put the bugle nonchalantly to my lips and blow real mellow tones. The whole place seems to change. Satisfied with my tone Mr. Davis gave me a cornet and taught me how to play 'Home, Sweet Home.'"[50]

Armstrong in the Waifs Home Band
(Louis Armstrong House and Museum)

---

[49] Armstrong, *Satchmo: My Life in New Orleans*, 38.
[50] Louis Armstrong, *Satchmo: My Life in New Orleans*, 46.

Booker Washington's influence on Black educational philosophy and economic matters was far and wide. George Schuyler was a Washington devotee who thought Negro art was nonexistent, and though Captain Jones may have shared Schuyler's patriotic attitude, it was clear that he encouraged visual and performing arts as integral parts of the Colored Boys Waifs Home's curriculum. At his behest, and under Mr. Peter Davis's tutelage, the reformatory band was a success. Indeed, the performing arts activity included an element of vocal music, as both were extracurricular components of the institution's curriculum, and the band regularly performed in community parades. Indeed, Captain Jones embraced the importance of unique cultural behaviors (parades were integral to New Orleans culture) just as Langston Hughes suggested years later it in his landmark essay, "The Negro Artist and the Racial Mountain." Armstrong alluded to Jones's importance to his development beyond music on several occasions, particularly when his career was ascending during the 1930s.[51] Therefore, it is essential to explore the source of Jones's patriotism, dedication to civility, and most importantly, his sense of duty where the underserved children of New Orleans were concerned. Jones's attitude was indicative of a growing desire among many black leaders that African Americans are contributors to American culture, worthy of constitutional guarantees heretofore denied to them. The headmaster's patriotism was evident even during his retirement from military duty as the nation prepared for entry into World War I.

Captain Jones's sincere patriotism inspired him to (much to the successful chagrin of his wife) join the new Black officer training corps arranged by the War Department through the efforts of W. E. B. Du Bois and others. This writer explores the subject in more detail in a subsequent chapter. Specifically, during the period leading to America's decision to participate in World War I (which was coincidently the years just before the Harlem Renaissance), Du Bois advocated for black participation.[52] The leader embraced black involvement in the war

---

[51] See George W. Kay's Forward to "Louis Armstrong's Letter to His Daddy," *The Second Line* Hogan Jazz Archives, 1976, Tulane University, New Orleans, LA, 12–15.

[52] See David Levering Lewis's discussion of Du Bois's quest for a black officer training school in *W. E. B. Du Bois: Biography of a Race 1868–1919* (New York:

effort as a means of proving patriotism and advancing the push for constitutionally guaranteed freedoms. He successfully pushed for the creation of the nations' first Black officer training corps. Many in the African American community agreed that this was an opportunity to demonstrate patriotism. Joseph W. Holley and the Albany Bible and Manual Training Institute too embraced the patriotic mood. Holley, the male students, and faculty volunteered for military service.[53] Jones, Du Bois, and Holley believed military service would be an affirmation of their patriotism, proving them worthy of constitutional guarantees. The years following the war were fraught with racial tension.

Efforts to get Congress to pass an antilynching bill failed, and Black resistance and retaliation to then perpetual oppression rose (evident in the riots during the summer of 1919). The New Negro sentiment (which this writer will explore further in Chapter V) expressed in DuBois's essay, *Returning Soldiers* and Claude McKay's *If We Must Die* was prevalent.[54] However, Armstrong's career was antithetical. His years as an apprentice turned into opportunities to grow as an artist while often exploring collective improvisation in a blues music setting. He evolved artistically from a sideman in some of New Orleans's top venues to a leader replacing his idol Joe "King" Oliver. The latter relocated to Chicago, as did many African Americans during a wave of migration. His stint on the Mississippi River riverboat Sydney allowed for growth as a reading musician. However, Armstrong's eventual move to Chicago at the behest of Oliver to join the latter's band proved to be prophetic, as the young blues and jazz artist attained wide-range recognition for his improvisational skills.

In 1924, Armstrong joined fellow New Orleanian, Sidney Bechet, Charles Irvis, and pianist Clarence Williams to record "Texas Moaner Blues" (see Figure 2). The wind instruments in this aggregation, clarinet (Bechet), trumpet (Armstrong), and trombone (Irvis) were commonplace

---

Henry Holt and Company, 1993), 555–567.
[53] See Holley's discussion regarding the male faculty and students volunteering for World War I in *You Can't Build a Chimney from the Top*, 31–2.
[54] See Claude McKay's epic poem, "If We Must Die," *The Portable Harlem Renaissance Reader*, ed. David Levering Lewis (New York: Penguin Books 1994), 289.

in a traditional New Orleans jazz band. The significance here is that the melody prevails while improvisational freedom is not only sought but expected. Armstrong, Bechet, and Irvis juxtaposed the timbre of each instrument with polyrhythmic sensibilities reminiscent of the instrumental blues music they heard in New Orleans. The musicians understood the roles of their instruments just as the Congo Square performing artists did almost a century earlier exercises while recalling the of their native homeland, accompanying dancers and inspiring vocalists.[55] Their comprehension of creating blues music in a traditional New Orleans jazz ensemble elevates the recording into a performance that ranks as seminal in this writer's point of view. Though relatively early in their careers, Armstrong and Bechet are well-versed in the blues tradition, musical clichés, and the genre's instrumental vernacular.[56] The success of their stop-time explorations, the shifting roles (Armstrong's choices in the second chorus), and completion of the collective musicianship (Bechet's mastery of improvising a solo on soprano saxophone while maintaining intonation and character on both it and the clarinet) make this a seminal recording. Bechet's and Armstrong's improvisational art, as well Williams's leadership and Irvis's musical sensibilities make this a seminal recording in the period's blues music lexicon.

Sidney Bechet (Schomburg Center, New York Public Library)

---

[55] See Bechet's discussion of timbre and the traditional New Orleans brass band in his autobiography, *Treat It Gentle*, 85–94.

[56] Armstrong and Bechet had extensive training in the blues tradition while coming of age as performing artists in New Orleans. The artists often refer to learning to play the "blues" in their memoir and autobiography (*Satchmo: My Life in New Orleans*, 64–71 and *Treat It Gentle*, 89–93).

Figure 2

Texas Moaner Blues

F. Barnes and C. Williams
Transcribed By: Michael Decuir

(continued)

(continued)

(continued)

Texas Moaner Blues

Further analysis of the wind instruments in this recording (Figure 2) unveils three aspects prevalent in West African and African American music: (a) antiphonal effects, (b) rhythmic contrasts, and (c) call response. The former is evident in the role Bechet takes in the first chorus. After an initial musical statement by Irvis, Bechet offers a brief response while maintaining the traditional function of the clarinetist. A combination of the three musical practices exists over the next four measures as Bechet does not wait until Irvis's statement is complete before making his musical reply.

Figure 2. Louis Armstrong's, Sidney Bechet's, and Charles Irvis's rendition of "Texas Moaner Blues"

His line continues to accompany Irvis's musical statement and is not completed until three full beats after Irvis has come to rest at measure number nineteen. Though Bechet's line is long and expressive, it maintains the established responsorial characteristic. In this setting, and thus context, Bechet's improvised musical response is a reaction to the music played earlier.

In response to Bechet, and while imitative of the New Orleans wind-instrument blues music tradition, Armstrong assumes the role of the trombonist in measure number twenty. His response is supportive as he fills in the space with the sensitivity of a seasoned blues musician. Armstrong occupies the space left when Bechet completes his response.[57] His artistic choices here represent a courageous endeavor allowing for rhythmical differentiation which in turn gives the listener a sense of double-time (faster) feeling that is not there. Evident as Bechet's entrance arrives on the upbeat of beat number four. Blues composer/theorist and Harlem Renaissance entrepreneur, W. C. Handy believed African American music contained two key elements: "The first of these is a marked insistent syncopation. The second is the novel element of filling in breaks."[58] Handy elaborated further when discussing the latter:

> The Negro becomes impatient with silences, and fills in the rests-spaces with impromptu embellishments of his own. He slips in an 'OH Lawdy!' before the next regular beat is due. These natural improvisations are the foundations of Jazz... The grandson of the old gang worker who put in a simple 'Oh Lawdy' fills in with both virtuosity on the saxophone; but both are expressing the identical racial instinct in a typically racial way."[59]

Bechet's solo, (see Figure 2) in measure number thirty-six begins with the "novel" practice of filling up space and then proceeds to utilize responsorial effects with each measure while displaying rhythmic differentiation with superb articulation. The character established in the previous measures changes when he plays connecting musical phrases while bending notes with the distinctive Bechet vibrato. Bechet's soprano saxophone solo also has vestiges of another aspect of West African

---

[57] See measures twenty and twenty-two in Figure 2.
[58] William Christopher Handy, "The Heart of the Blues." *Etude Music Magazine* March, 1940, 152.
[59] Ibid., 152.

musical practices. Specifically, Bechet plays the first three measures with the intent of a responsorial effect. Similarly, Olly Wilson surmises similar a West African musical practice: "There seems to be a profusion of musical activities going on simultaneously, as if an attempt is being made to fill up every available area of musical space."[60] When Bechet's solo changes character an African American blues music approach is evident.

Wilson notes that approach with regards to performance art practices, "It is a well-known fact that the performance technique a black jazz musician uses is not the same as that of his white symphonic counterpart and that this distinct manner of playing an instrument as of the voice has been a unique Afro-American feature throughout history."[61] Wilson's description here precisely describes the separation and fascination with Black American performing art during the period considered here.

Armstrong's artistry in "Texas Moaner Blues" served as a pretense to the collective improvisation on display in Armstrong's Hot Five and Hot Seven bands during the rest of the decade.[62] In this writer's opinion, the recording helped to elevate the artistry of the traditional New Orleans jazz band's practice of collective improvisation in a blues setting. Beyond the previous recordings of the Original Dixieland Jazz Band, King Oliver's Creole Jazz Band, and Freddie Keppard, 'Texas Moaner Blues" served as a landmark for the performance of jazz and blues music. Finally, what is of significant note here is that vestiges of Armstrong's art are evident in subsequent American music genres, rhythm and blues, rock and roll, soul, hard rock, and funk.

---

[60] Olly Wilson, "The Significance of African and African-American Music," *Black Perspectives in Music* 2, no. 1 (Spring, 1974): 15.

[61] Ibid.

[62] Armstrong recorded "Texas Moaner Blues" in New York then returned to Chicago and formed the Hot Five and Hot Seven bands, which are famous for recordings "Black and Blue" and "West End Blues."

CHAPTER III

LOUIS ARMSTRONG, W. E. B. DU BOIS, AND THE BUSINESS OF BLUES MUSIC DURING THE HARLEM RENAISSANCE

On July 16, 1930, Louis Armstrong traveled to Los Angeles, California, and recorded "Blue Yodel No. 9" as a sideman. The event was otherwise insignificant as the artist had served in the same capacity 114 times over the previous seven years. However, the Los Angeles date was a milestone of sorts. Armstrong was accompanying the iconic White-American country music pioneer Jimmie Rodgers. The significance here is that to the detriment of the growth of many White artists in the blues and jazz music genres, rarely did Black and White musicians rehearse, perform, or record together. Racially integrated musical aggregations and performances were both outlawed in the South and frowned upon in most other parts of the country. In the context of Armstrong's career, the event served as the culmination of a body of work during the Harlem Renaissance that was transforming American music as the cultural arts period was coming to an end. It also served as the commencement to forty years of instrumental and vocal performing choices that codified stylistic choices in future American music idioms.

Jimmie Rodgers was an emerging country music star who embraced the art of making blues music, explicitly, in its twelve-bar form. A form that is conducive for improvisation, a skill Armstrong mastered during the years before the recording. By 1926, the ascension of the popularity of blues music was measurable when placed in the context of record sales. Simultaneously, the discussion of the worth, purpose, and existence of the period's arts was elevating. Interestingly, Armstrong's growth from his earliest records ("Chimes Blues" in 1923 and "Texas Moaner Blues" in 1924) to the period's seminal recordings, "Black and Blue" and "West End Blues" in 1926 and 1928 respectively, parallels the rise in blues and jazz music's popularity between 1923 and 1930.[63] His contributions are the culmination of social and cultural experiences as a child and adolescent in New Orleans, where the performing arts in the Black community was primarily an agglutination of African American folk music (blues and ragtime), with the West African musical practices exhibited by the enslaved in Congo Square. To this end, Armstrong's art and the popularity of blues and jazz music helped to inspire a debate as to the quiddity, purpose, and legitimacy of the Harlem Renaissance. The discussion's participants included some of the period's salient artists, activists, and theorists.

A review of W. E. B. Du Bois's 1926 speech to the National Association for the Advancement of Colored People, titled "The Criteria of Negro Art," shows his awareness of the ascending popularity of the arts in the African American community and its potential impact on political thought and inspiration for social activism. He believed African American art should unabashedly embrace all aspects of Black life, including the Jim Crow South and the oppressive North. Du Bois said, "The apostle of Beauty thus becomes the apostle of Truth and Right not by choice but by inner and outer compulsion. Free he is but his freedom is ever bounded by Truth and Justice; and slavery only dogs him when he is denied the right to tell the Truth or recognize an ideal

---

[63] Figure 1 illustrates Armstrong's contributions and some of the seminal events of the period considered here.

of Justice."[64] Du Bois also thought that only by shedding light on the inequities in Black life, juxtaposed with the bravery shown by African American soldiers in World War I, will the nation's power structure be alarmed enough to affect change. Cultural theorist Alain Locke held a contrary view. He believed that any art based solely upon racial themes is detrimental to any goal of broader acceptance in a dominant culture. Specifically, Locke thought art as propaganda is boring and conforms to the opinion prevalent in the Eurocentric critical arena. Specifically, many critics believed that the artistic works of African American artists were subpar because they were incapable of creating works that would meet Eurocentric standards. In 1926 Locke wrote, "My chief objection to propaganda, apart from its besetting sin of monotony and disproportion, that it perpetuates the position of group inferiority even in crying out against it."[65] Interestingly, the two shared an optimism regarding the talent and possibilities of the period's young artists.

According to Du Bois,

> We black folk may help for we have within us as a race new stirring; stirrings of the beginning of a new appreciation of joy, of a new desire to create, of a new will to be; as though in this morning of group life we had awakened from sleep that at once dimly mourns the past and dreams a splendid future; and there has come the conviction that the Youth that his here today, the Negro Youth, is a different kind of Youth, because in some new way it bears this mighty prophecy on its breast, with a new realization of itself, with determination for all mankind.[66]

---

[64] Du Bois's admonitions are implicit in the text of his 1926 speech to the National Association for the Advancement of Colored People, titled "The Criteria of Negro Art."
[65] Alain Locke, "Art or Propaganda," *Harlem* Vol. I (November 1928): 219, 256.
[66] Ibid.

Locke opined,

> With this renewed self-respect and self-dependence, the life of the Negro community is bound to enter a new dynamic phase, the buoyancy from within compensating for whatever pressure there may be of conditions from without. The migrant masses, shifting from country-side to city, hurdle several generations of experience at a leap, but more important, the same thing happens spiritually in the life-attitudes and self-expression of the Young Negro, in his poetry, his art, his education and his out-look, with the additional advantage, of course, of the poise and greater certainty knowing what it is all about.[67]

The audacity and tenacity of the period's Black American artists served as the impetus for Du Bois's and Locke's opinions. Two of the period's seminal figures, critic George Schuyler and poet Langston Hughes had expressed opposite views on the matter. The pair's opposing views of the period's arts were indicative of the contemporaneous debate regarding the role and mode of education of Blacks, particularly in the South. Schuyler, a Booker T. Washington devotee, believed in the industrial education model. Hughes was so impressed with Du Bois, that he wrote a poem titled "I've Known Rivers" and dedicated it to the leader. Whether an Blacks should experience an industrial (agricultural studies, domestic sciences, mechanics, carpentry) education, or a college-prep curriculum with the arts, math, social studies, foreign language, and the sciences—were at its core.

---

[67] Locke, *The New Negro* (New York: 1925)

W. E. B. Du Bois   Alain Locke
(Schomburg Center, New York Public Library)

There has been a persistent sentiment in the curriculums and the Western art canon that promulgates the myth that knowledge, civility, and the act of pondering the existence of a creator are all gifts brought to Africa by northern visitors whose purpose was to endow the continent's inhabitants with such knowledge. Consequently, Western art curricula emulate a Eurocentric or colonial point of view and systematically excludes or minimizes most accomplishments and contributions to world history and culture by Africans and African Americans. Cultural theorist Amiri Baraka opined, "But one of the most persistent traits of the Western white man has always been his fanatical and almost instinctive assumption that his systems and ideas about the world are the most desirable, and further, that people who do not aspire to them, or at least think them admirable, are savages or enemies."[68] Baraka's theory strikes at the heart of the matter regarding the Eurocentric resistance to multicultural infusion into curricula.

Baraka's conjecture is evident in most discussions of the period researched here. The discussion reverberates contemporaneously in the debate as to the inclusiveness or exclusiveness of Black studies in secondary and postsecondary curricula. In the performing arts, the Eurocentric model for education is apparent as courses such as music appreciation utilize textbooks that give little attention to the

---

[68] Amiri Baraka, *Blues People: Negro Music in White America* (New York: Harper Collins Books, 1963), 29.

accomplishments African Americans on the period's performing artists. Conversely, Eurocentric musicologists readily acknowledge the impact of particular performing Western artists by placing them in a historical context.[69] Specifically, theorists do not hesitate to credit or attach a specific performing arts genre to a relative corresponding date of existence or style, movement, or cultural period. Western art music historians designate historical periods—Baroque, Classical, Romantic, and Modern eras—as musical periods. The visual and literary arts created during those prescribed timelines are readily juxtaposed with the relative music. To this end, the failure to acknowledge non-Western contributions to Western art served to normalize the marginalization of the importance of the Harlem Renaissance.

The period's performing artists, notably Louis Armstrong, did not escape the lack of recognition. This was evident even in publications that extolled the virtues of the period. In the foreword to Nathan Irvin Huggins's salient publication, *Harlem Renaissance*, Arnold Rampersad wrote, "One of the lesser strengths of this book—one can lodge this complaint about every book in existence about the Harlem Renaissance— is the treatment of music, although what Huggins writes about blues and jazz is certainly more than adequate as a contribution to the mainstream of his arguments."[70] Rampersad's thoughts reveal the all-too-often practice of separating or minimizing the importance of the performing arts to the period considered here. To place blues and jazz music in the context of their significance to the period, one must explore Armstrong's choices, other significant artists, salient recordings, and their impact upon the period's economics.

Composer, performing artist, and cultural theorist W. C. Handy displayed a keen business sense along with a degree of musicological instincts during the decade leading to and including the Harlem Renaissance. Years earlier, while living in the South, he recognized the power of blues music and its potential as a business. Interestingly,

---

[69] Donald Jay Grout's, *A History of Western Music* (New York: Norton, 1960) is a widely used textbook in American music programs.

[70] Arnold Rampersad, Forward to *Harlem Renaissance,* Nathan Irvin Huggins (New York: Oxford University Press 2007), xxx.

Booker T. Washington's admonitions may have inspired Handy. In his autobiography *Up From Slavery*, Booker T. Washington advocated for the creation of a Negro Business League. The organization's mission was to establish a commercial infrastructure in the African American community dedicated to economic empowerment. According to Washington,

> In the summer of 1900 with the assistance of such prominent colored men as T. Thomas Fortune, who has always upheld my hands in every effort, I organized the National Negro Business League, which held its first meeting in Boston, and brought together for the first time a large number of coloured men who are engaged in various lines of trade or business in different parts of the United States.[71]

By the time of his death in 1915 and at the dawn of the latest New Negro sentiment, Washington was arguably one of the leading Black American voices on education and black commerce. The former slave believed that successfully controlling the monetary ebb and flow via Negro entrepreneurship was the surest mode to freedom. Mirroring Washington's sentiments, an African American entrepreneur, Harry Pace, joined blues music progenitors, Clarence Williams and W.C. Handy, to form a publishing and recording company called Black Swan Records.[72] Under their leadership, the genre continued an aesthetic ascendance in American

William C. Handy

---

[71] Booker T. Washington, *Up from Slavery* (New York: Penguin Books, 2000), 222.
[72] See Eileen Southern's discussion of the Pace Recording Company in *The Music of Black Americans* (New York: W.W. Norton & Company, 1997), 370–71.

culture. The company successfully recruited and recorded blues writers and performing artists. Handy alone authored hundreds of songs, including "St. Louis Blues" and "Memphis Blues." Subsequently, sales and performances of blues music rose steadily between 1923 and the stock market crash of 1929. Armstrong's art (instrumental and vocal) was heard increasingly during the same years as he recorded in an accompanying role 114 times during those years. Researcher Gilbert Erskine surmised, "It is no secret that Louis Armstrong did some of his best playing accompanying singers on recordings in the 1920s."[73]

Harry Pace and W. C. Handy established themselves in the music-publishing business. The former established the Pace Recording Company after the partnership's dissolution in 1921. Pace then created the Black Swan Record label. Impresario, and New Orleans native Clarence Williams who wrote and produced "Texas Moaner Blues" (referred to in the first chapter of this research), joined forces with Pace and the two successfully recruited Fletcher Henderson and William Grant Still (who later became one of America's significant twentieth-century composers) to join the label's writing and production team. Harlem Renaissance singer and Black Swan recording artist Ethel Waters described signing with the company and meeting Pace and Handy: "The same talent scout who dug me up for Cardinal (Recording Company) worked for other record companies. After catching my act at Edmond's (a Harlem night spot) a second time, he asked if I would care to make some records for Black Swan, a new company just started by Harry H. Pace and W. C. Handy, the two grand old men of Negro music."[74] Eileen Southern described the label's accomplishment: "The Black Swan's repertory consisted of light classical pieces, spirituals, blues, ballads, piano and violin solos, and character songs."[75] The recording

---

[73] Gilbert Erskine, "'Countin' the Blues: A Survey of the Recordings Of Louis Armstrong Accompanying Singers In The 1920s,'" *The Second Line*, Hogan Jazz Archives, Tulane University, (Spring 1976): 10.

[74] Ethel Waters and Charles Samuel, *His Eye Is on the Sparrow* (New York: Doubleday & Co., 1950), 141–42.

[75] Eileen Southern, *The Music of Black Americans*, 371.

company's artistic choices are indicative of their attitude to present black music talent beyond just blues and jazz music.

Armstrong's increasing number of recordings as an accompanist is a testimony to the growing respect for his artistry and the recognition of his popularity. Certainly, many indicators contributed to the rise in the popularity of blues and jazz music. Notably, the performing arts' rise in popularity correlated with the subsequent influence on the period's literary, visual, and performing arts. The availability of radios and phonographs to not only middle- and upper-income families, but also to low-income citizens, was a contributing factor. Many, if not most, were becoming employed in industries that supported the war effort and beyond. Indeed, the migration to major industrial centers such as Chicago, Detroit, Cleveland, and New York played a significant role in the cultural shift. Significantly, the human instinct to bring mores, folkways, and indeed the music from one region to a new one is not uncommon for a group. Researcher Elijah Wald said, "Ever since the Civil War, black southerners have been leaving the country-side and heading for urban areas, crowding the booming black districts of Dallas, Memphis, and Atlanta. After World War I, this trend was greatly accelerated, and by the 1930s, most of these emigrants were heading for industrial centers farther north: St. Louis, Detroit, Chicago, and New York."[76] There existed among many Southern African Americans a desire to escape the oppressive claws of the Jim Crow South, which bound them and their posterity to denial of constitutional rights, increased organized terrorist activities, and limited educational opportunities. Violence juxtaposed with no legal protection from governing authorities were the rewards for resistance to the cyclical, oppressive system called sharecropping, and performing or listening to blues music became a coping mechanism. Period researcher David Levering Lewis offered this statistical analysis of the population shift:

---

[76] Elijah Wald, *Escaping the Delta: Robert Johnson and the Invention of the Blues* (New York: HarperCollins Publishers, Inc. 2004), 38.

Chicago's Afro-American population increased in the decade after 1910 to 1920 by 148.2 percent, most of the migrants arriving after 1917. There was a similar increase in Detroit, where migrants from the South swelled the Afro-American population by no less than 611.3 percent; Indianapolis, 59 percent; Cincinnati, 53.2 percent; Pittsburgh, 47.2 percent. Three hundred thousand, and possibly many more, Afro-American farmers, unskilled laborers, and domestics left the South before 1920.[77]

The change in the region's demographics, which incidentally preempted radio's popularity, meant a shift in cultural behaviors, aesthetics, and musical choices in the northern industrial areas. Historian Patrick Manning opined: "As another example of how cultural and social categories interact, with the end of slavery blacks were able to take control of their role as subordinated performers, which led to a burst in creativity throughout the black world."[78]

Harlem did not escape what was to some a cultural awakening. However, to others, the music was a recollection of an oppressive life in the South. Still others embraced the performing art as a means for instinctive creativity. To this end, World War I veterans and mainstays in James Reese Europe's band, Noble Sissle and Eubie Blake, contributed to the period's art. Sissle and Blake's creation was on display when in 1921, they wrote the music and lyrics to a Black musical on Broadway show titled *Shuffle Along*. Researcher Eileen Southern said, "*Shuffle Along* brought a 'different' kind of musical to Broadway, a Harlem folk show in which few concessions were made to white taste or to theater clichés."[79]

The period's black music theater musical genre produced some of America's seminal twentieth-century musicians. They included Paul Robeson, Florence Mills, Josephine Baker, and Caterina Jarboro, among

---

[77] David Levering Lewis, *When Harlem Was in Vogue* (New York: Penguin Books, 1997), 20.

[78] Patrick Manning, *The African Diaspora: A History Through Culture* (New York: Columbian University Press, 2010), 25.

[79] Eileen Southern, *The Music of Black Americans*, 436.

others. Some of the other significant Black theatrical productions and the chief composers who performed on and off-Broadway were *Liza,* Maceo Pinkard (1922); *Runnin Wild,* James P. Johnson (1923); *Chocolate Dandies,* Eubie Blake and Spencer Williams (1924); *Africana,* Donald Heywood (1927); *Hot Chocolates* Walter and Harry Brooks (1929); and *Brown Buddies,* Joe Jordan (1930). Despite such artistic activity, period detractors openly questioned the validity of an African American art movement.

A glimpse into the commercial potential of blues music at the dawn of the period considered here reveals that the commencement of the 1920s gave rise to a surge in the interest in Blues Music as a possible business venture. Indeed, the OKeh recording company was one of the earliest organizations to capitalize on the attraction of Southern African American folk music. Researcher L. A. Jackson notes OKeh's success after Mamie Smith's 1920 recording of *Crazy Blues*: "1920 recording of *Crazy Blues* by black composer Perry Bradford was released on the legendary OKeh label. *Crazy Blues* jump started the 'race record' industry (the term used for records aimed at black consumers) and things were never the same again, as average sales of this music climbed to 5 million units a year."[80]

By 1926, Columbia Records bought the company and began capitalizing on field recordings emanating from rural areas of the South. The company also turned to Louis Armstrong's improvisational skills to help lend a degree of legitimacy and quality to signed artists. Despite the music business's capital gains, the period's critics such as George Schuyler did not sway. He continued to insist that the literary, performing, and visual arts produced by African American artists were nonexistent or, at the least, figments of white consumer fantasies. Though he (Schuyler) did not specifically mention Louis Armstrong or other artists, his criticisms lay bare the period detractor's point of view.

Schuyler expressed a contrary point of view in a 1926 essay titled "The Negro Art-Hokum," Schuyler believed that the period's literary

---

[80] L.A. Jackson, ed. Anna R. Holloway, PhD., *Musicology 2101: A Quick Start Guide to Music Biz History* (Atlanta: MKM Publishing, 2010), 111.

and visual arts were, in fact, subpar and lacked any cultural distinction. However, he extricated the performing arts from the discussion. Subsequently, from a contrarian point of view, he ignored the impact of blues music on contemporary American culture. Interestingly, in his autobiography, *Black and Conservative*, Schuyler even boasted (possibly from a serendipitous point of view) of often hearing blues artists in various Harlem venues. He described his experiences as such:

> Of course the principal fare offered was vaudeville, and the best Negro Variety artists were billed. It was there that I first heard Mamie Smith singing the blues, and many of the best musicians of the day. Fats Waller played the organ at the Lincoln and on Seventh Avenue near West 135th Street, Pace and Handy had an office for their Black Swan Records, which are now collectors items much sought after by jazz fans.[81]

Later that same year, literary artist Langston Hughes responded to Schuyler with an essay titled "The Negro Artist and the Racial Mountain." A textual analysis of Hughes's article reveals that, contrary to Schuyler, he believed Black artists should embrace their blackness and not be afraid to use the viscidness and idiosyncrasies of life in America as a conduit for expression and advocacy.

---

[81] George Schuyler, *Black and Conservative* (New York: Arlington House Publishers, 1966) 125.

Langston Hughes   George Schuyler
(Schomburg Center, New York Public Library)

Complicating matters of cultural acknowledgement was the disdain held by many Black Americans for Armstrong's stage presence. Many rejected his art because of a contemptuous attitude developed from a real and perceived disdain for nineteenth-century minstrel caricatures that continued to permeate the American culture during the first three decades of the twentieth century. Critics associated Armstrong's demeanor on stage with images from nineteenth-century minstrel shows. Armstrong emulated and enhanced the music of the jazz pioneers (many of whom were one or two generations removed from the Congo Square musicians) he saw in New Orleans with a high degree of technique and creativity. He nurtured an onstage presence as an extension of his art. Smiles and humble mannerisms were acts of recruiting consumers to partake the performing art and thus make the music making communal, further emulating the New Orleans and West African custom. Armstrong opined on the music's creative and geographical importance: "You know this music is art. But it's got to be art because the world has recognized our music from New Orleans, else it would have been dead today."[82] To the contrary, Schuyler chose to ignore the contributions African Americans such as the "Charleston dance," blues, ragtime, and jazz, and insisted that period performing (thus Armstrong's), literary, and visual arts were devoid of any connection to Afrocentricity. He surmised, "But these are contributions of a caste in a certain section of the country.

---

[82] *Louis Armstrong—A Self Portrait*, 58

They are foreign to Northern Negroes, West Indian Negroes, and African Negroes. They are no more expressive or characteristic of the Caucasian race."[83] Both ends of the continuum those who related his artistic choices to vestiges of Afrocentric culture and those who ere likely to disagree as to whether Armstrong's art and Blues Music had a bearing on the debate. Schuyler and others ignored not only the West African roots to the period's performing arts but also the childhood and adolescent years.

Much of Armstrong's childhood influences were the result of the economic pressures present in most of the second and third generations of postslavery families. Social choices that resulted in pernicious behaviors are not to be romanticized or excused. Importantly, many period critics noted that Armstrong often referred to the importance and impact of said harmful behaviors (gambling, prostitution, and drug usage) while coming of age in New Orleans. Nevertheless, the challenge of documenting Louis Armstrong's artistic contributions to the Harlem Renaissance requires qualitative analysis (see Figure 1). Therefore, it is necessary that a careful exploration of not only the popularity of blues music and Armstrong's contribution to the genre's acceptance in America but also its existence as a functional art created to eliminate or cope with life's maladies, such as those Armstrong experienced. Indeed, Armstrong and all the period's artists had the temerity to create in an era that simultaneously encouraged and codified their creative instincts.

Armstrong's art attracted increasing notoriety when his career began to skyrocket after 1923 with the release of "Chimes Blues." His accompanying choices and, to a degree, his improvisational choices while serving as Joe "King" Oliver's sideman caused

---

[83] George Schuyler, "The Negro-Art Hokum" in *The Nation* (New York: June 26, 1926).

a stir among fellow musicians and blues lovers alike. The musicians began to embrace the possibilities of improvisation as the impetus for jazz music. Simultaneously, consumer aesthetics increasingly gravitated to Blues and Jazz Music. Cultural theorist Thomas Dewey described the phenomena as the "perceiver must create his own experience. And his creation must include relations comparable to those which the original producer underwent."[84]

Dewey's theory is apparent in the literary art of Langston Hughes, James Weldon Johnson, and others. Similarly, period visual artists Aaron Douglass, Romare Bearden, Archibald Motley Jr., Roland Barthe, Meta Warrick Fuller, and others not only recognized but also created art that captured the depth of the period's cultural indicators. Indeed, the performance of jazz and blues music in varied venues inspired much of the artist's depictions (See Figure 1).

Blues music became more than a unifying aesthetic. It also functioned as art through which the maladies of everyday life, particularly for African Americans, can be identified or acknowledged through lyrics. The power to begin the process of liberation after identifying problems with one's life was also not lost on literary and visual artists.[85] Though Du Bois did not mention blues music specifically, he used his 1926 NAACP Convention keynote address to encourage Black artists to use their creations as tools to agitate for equality as well as an exposé on Black life in America. According to Du Bois, "All art is propaganda and ever must be, despite the wailing of the purists."[86] Indeed, Du Bois's admonitions helped ignite a debate about the role of the period's art. Predictably, Schuyler adopted a contrary view. He thought that Negro art, as such, was parochial at best and had no place in the pantheon of American culture. Theorists, like Schuyler, believed that African American culture was too far removed from any West African

---

[84] Thomas Dewey, *Art as Experience* (New York: Capricorn Books, 1959), 54.
[85] This writer became aware of blues music's role as a liberating force in Black American life from musician Branford Marsalis in *Jazz: A Film by Ken Burns* (Episode One, Gumbo, 2000).
[86] 84 W. E. B. Du Bois, "The Criteria of Negro Art," *Crisis Magazine* (October 1926): 10–11.

influences and, therefore, devoid of any African or ethnic uniqueness. Period researcher George Hutchinson agrees with Schuyler's West African/African American theory regarding the sources of Black art. He expressed the prevailing sentiment of Black culture as it relates to its uniqueness: "More important than the idea of the traditional 'Africaness' of African American culture to the Harlem Renaissance was the idea that Black Americans, unlike any other group, had been almost completely stripped of their ancestral cultural identity, and precisely because of this had developed the most authentically American folk culture."[87] Jazz researcher Sidney Finkelstein's admonitions reflect Hutchinson's reasoning. Finkelstein's theories. The historical data discussed, "Jazz is not even 'Afro-American,' a term comparatively new and popular among jazz theoreticians. To use such a hyphenated term implies that there are two Americas."[88]

Beyond Finkelstein's disregard for the affinity of many groups in this country to embrace "hyphenated terms" as a display of ethnic pride, he too dismisses the African origins inherent in jazz and blues music. This research seeks to disprove Schuyler and Finkelstein's theories. The research discussed in the first chapter reveals that the contributions from West Africa to world culture, the vestiges of performing art practices (call response, communal music making, and stratified rhythms) considered here, were present in Congo Square, and are the foundations of jazz and blues music.

Harlem Renaissance literary artist, Langston Hughes, adopted a contrary view to Schuyler's. He embraced the concept of using racial identity when creating art. Months after Schuyler's publication, "The Negro Art-Hokum," Hughes wrote an opposing view to the Black conservative's opinions, "The Negro Artist and the Racial Mountain." A comparative analysis of Schuyler's and Hughes's 1926 essays reveals contrasting views. Schuyler did not see any artistic value in "Negro art," and any desire to categorize blues and jazz music as distinctly African

---

[87] George Hutchinson, *The Harlem Renaissance in Black and White* (Cambridge: Harvard University Press 1995), 76.
[88] Ibid., 19.

American is foolhardy. Schuyler's position is that any ethnic group would have experienced similar cultural successes and identifying such accomplishment (mainly Black music) in ethnic contexts, increases the difficulty of being accepted into the dominant (American) culture.

Hughes, on the other hand, embraced the ethnic pride that inspired "Negro art," and in the context of the period considered here held contrary views to those striving for acceptance by mainstream American culture. In "The Negro Artist and the Racial Mountain," Hughes extolled the virtues and vicissitudes of African American culture as well as encouraged its use in Black art. In this context, Hughes admonished a young Black writer to resist those who urged him or her to avoid African American themes and acknowledged the talents of fellow period writer, Jean Toomer: "Both would have told Jean Toomer not to write *Cane*."[89] Hughes commented further, "They are afraid of it. Although the critics gave it good reviews, the public remained indifferent. Yet (excepting for the work of Du Bois) Cane contains the finest prose written by a Negro in America. And like the singing of Robeson, it is racial."[90] Hughes's prognostications were both accurate and foretelling.

Despite efforts to forget, Black American music reminded the period's detractors of life in postslavery South under an oppressive Jim Crow existence. Often, spirituals, field hollers, work songs, and blues music, served as tools for coping. To this end, one of the critical aspects of the rituals and mores in New Orleans is the inescapable presence of cultural behaviors whose roots lie in the practices of the enslaved and free people of color in the region. The impact of these cultural behaviors (communal music making, stratified or polyrhythms, and contextualized improvisational freedom) on American music was as significant as any other performing art. The reader may recall the earlier discussion in the first chapter regarding the significant presence and access to operas, and other Eurocentric performance arts in the city. Armstrong codified the area's unique approach to the performing arts

---

[89] Hughes, "The Negro Artist and the Racial Mountain," *The Nation* CXXII (June 1926): 290–97.
[90] Ibid.

and gave the world a variety of trumpet solos indicative of the period's artistry. Indeed, the artist had an extraordinary ability to appropriate the New Orleans early jazz wind-instrument polyphony (particularly their roles) in recordings from 1924 "Texas Moaner Blues" to the 1962 collaboration with Edward "Duke" Ellington, "Solitude." Significantly, and pertinent to Armstrong's influence on the genre's popularity, blues recording artists Ma Rainey, Bessie Smith, and Ethel Waters recognized his improvisational prowess, and all used him as a sideman on their recordings.[91] Indeed, Armstrong's improvisational vocal music choices were just as impactful. He was one of the first male blues recording stars and fueled a rise in record sales.

Armstrong's vocal style was imitated just as much as his instrumental creations. More importantly, he developed his vocal instincts while coming of age in New Orleans submerged in the West African folkways and multicultural music.[92] His impact on Blues Music's popularity and record sales was born out of an artistic prowess that was developed a decade earlier on the streets of New Orleans. Early New Orleans jazz artists Sidney Bechet and Bunk Johnson noted his skills (at an early age) as a member of a singing group impressing those who heard them on the streets of the city. According to Bechet, "It was Bunk Johnson who was the first to make me acquainted with Louis Armstrong. Bunk told me about this quartet Louis was singing in. 'Sidney,' he said, 'I want you to go hear a little quartet, how they sing and harmonize."[93] The point here is that Armstrong and his group developed an ability to imitate instruments using syllabic inferences while maintaining a musical style reminiscent of ragtime music in the context of the aforementioned New Orleans wind-instrument polyphony.

It is a mistake to suppose this and other musical instincts of the period's artists (called "jungle" music) were the result of natural or

---

[91] See Terry Teachout's discussion regarding this matter in *Pops: A Life of Louis Armstrong* (Boston: Houghton Mifflin Harcourt, 2009), 89–92.

[92] The reader is encouraged to read Sidney Bechet's recollection of young Armstrong singing for tips with a quartet on the streets of New Orleans in his autobiography, *Treat It Gentle*.

[93] Bechet, *Treat It Gentle*

inherent ability, a mistake often made by the detractors. To this end, what we hear in Armstrong's early recordings, "Heebie Jeebies" to "Blue Yodel No. 9" is an existential art born of years of practice and street performances growing up in New Orleans. Researcher Vic Hobson's description of the quartet's harmonic approach is telling, particularly Armstrong's role. "In his barbershop quartet, Louis sang first tenor, and therefore he would have sung above Little Mack singing lead. This unlike a European quartet where lead is usually sung by the top voice."[94] There was an evolvement (codified instrumental roles, indoor-outdoor performance practices including their function as a part of funeral rituals) in New Orleans of the performing art known as jazz and blues music from the time of Armstrong's birth in 1901 to his departure in 1919. Black American music experienced a similar creative growth during the Harlem Renaissance as it helped inspire political and philosophical thought, as well as literary and visual art themes. Indeed, early twentieth-century New Orleans did not attract philosophers and literary and visual artists like Harlem. However, and arguably, the popularity of the live music scene and performing arts culture in New Orleans from 1900 to 1919 rivaled any municipality in the world.[95]

The period between 1900 and 1930 in Black America gave rise to artistic achievements, more profound identification of social ills and prescribed solutions, resulting in an unintended cultural agglutination. However, at times, the prescribed solutions directly conflicted with each other. Nowhere was the conflict-solution paradigm more evident than in the Booker T. Washington's and W. E. B. Du Bois's approach to solving the race problem in America.[96] This research seeks to describe each philosopher's thoughts including similarities and their impact on the period's philosophy, politics, and subsequently art. For example, Washington's influence on education at historically Black colleges is integral to the education debate. His industrial education ideas are the

---

[94] Vic Hobson, *Louis Armstrong and Barbershop Harmony: Creating the Jazz Solo* (Jackson: University Press of Mississippi, 2018), 13.
[95] See Armstrong's *Satchmo: My Life in New Orleans,* 211–40.
[96] See Du Bois's discussion regarding Washington's industrial education views in *The Souls of Black Folk,* 57–81.

foundation for institutions such as the Colored Waif's Home, where young Louis Armstrong spent several months and received formal music training.

Schuyler questioned not only the validity, but the very existence of a cultural arts movement in Harlem and America's Black community. He contemporaneously codified Washington's conservative values into criticism of the quest for Black art. Schuyler's criticism was threefold. He thought the period was nonexistent; its Black artists should produce art as mimeticists, and that they were under an illusion believing their creations were unique with distinctive African American features. According to Schuyler: "I argued that such performance by colored American artists would in the very nature of things be distinguishable from other American art; that the American Negro was a lampblacked [sic] Anglo-Saxon, and could no more escape the imprint of his environment than colored people in other lands had done."[97] Schuyler's attitude is indicative of the Eurocentric hermeneutical approach to the critique of art. He believed that Black artists were either imitators conforming to Eurocentric parameters for critical acceptance or opportunists expressing falsehoods to take advantage of a phantom, re-written history. Decades later, activist Paulo Freire suggested in *The Pedagogy of the Oppressed* that this is the result of a successful cultural invasion because "it is essential that those invaded become convinced of their intrinsic inferiority. Since everything has its opposite, if those who are invaded consider themselves inferior, they must necessarily recognize the superiority of the invaders."[98]

Paradoxically, Armstrong, as well as other Renaissance artists, fully embraced the collective experiences of being African American, similar to those claiming to promulgate the nationalistic fervor in Europe. In the spirit of a contrarian, Schuyler published his views as the period's performing arts were reaching their zenith. That same year, 1925, Armstrong's seminal recording of Fats Waller's "Black and Blue" was

---

[97] George Schuyler, *Black and Conservative: The Autobiography of George Schuyler* (New York: Arlington House Publishers, 1966), 157.

[98] Paulo Friere, *The Pedagogy of the Oppressed* (London: Penguin Books, 1993), 154.

released. Schuyler and critics of blues music failed to recognize the cultural impact and the collective African American aesthetic of not only blues music, but also the genius and revolution in Armstrong's art. Indeed, Armstrong's legacy is that his improvisational choices forever changed the music, particularly the individual artist's approach to making it.

By 1928, the year Armstrong recorded "West End Blues," blues music was already an iconic entity in the American folk song canon. It was indeed an integral part of American culture, and it helped create an economic boom in the music industry during the third decade of the twentieth century. The art was romanticized by many consumers as the music of a people who were far removed from the South (many migrated to northern urban areas like Harlem) and are musically recalling their earlier existence. African American folk art was, in reality, born from the recognition by Black musicians of the forces responsible for their stifling oppression, particularly in the Jim Crow South. Freire opined that one of the steps to liberation is recognizing who or what are the sources of oppression. "To surmount the situation of oppression, people must first recognize its causes, so that through transforming action they can create a new situation, one which makes possible the pursuit of a fuller humanity."[99] Armstrong's and other musicians' artistic choices, especially when playing blues music, are evidence of such recognition. Though relatively young, and in the commencement of a blossoming career, Armstrong had done over one hundred blues recordings with the likes of Bessie Smith, Sidney Bechet, and Joe "King" Oliver.[100] His recorded artistic choices between 1924 and 1928 were receiving as much critical acclaim as was his live performances. Though his art was in its skeletal stages of transforming American music, his critical acclaim was on a trajectory.

Armstrong and other Black artists were not beyond experiencing the oppression and bigotry that served as the impetus for the creation of blues music. In the context of Friere's theory on liberation, the period artists

---

[99] Ibid., 29.
[100] See Armstrong's discography as a sideman at the end of this research.

musically transformed their existence by rejecting the presubscribed "jungle music" image. According to Freire, the oppressed must, "eject the image and replace it with autonomy and responsibility. Freedom is acquired by conquest, not by gift."[101] Subsequently, in "West End Blues," Armstrong "internalized the oppressor" when he began with an introductory trumpet fanfare in the traditional Western art music setting.[102] After reaching a tonal zenith, his improvisation continued when he created a virtuoso melodic blues descent to the tonic, giving no hint of the dirge-like melody that followed.[103] His improvisational choices at that point were indicative of Friere's concept of an artist free from the "fear of freedom."

Many who might otherwise serve as the oppressing group benefitted from Armstrong's creative transformations attained from losing the "fear of freedom" as they increasingly consumed the art during the period. Freire stated, "Although the situation of oppression is a dehumanized and dehumanizing totality affecting both the oppressor and those of whom they oppress, it is the latter who must from their stifled humanity, wage for both the struggle for a fuller humanity…"[104] Blues music's popularity is indicative of Freire's theory. Specifically, Armstrong revolutionized vocal styles in a still-developing American songbook, giving the genre a much-needed nationalistic ambiance. While attending college in Texas, Charles Black, who became one of the White attorneys and legal architects of the NAACP's arguments in Brown v. Board of Education, heard Armstrong and was inspired to view race relations from the ironic paradigm, which suggests nobility present in an artist who despite experiencing the vicissitudes of oppression, produces art to such a magnitude. Armstrong was engaged in the struggle for a fuller humanity and those like Charles Black were the recipients.[105]

---

[101] Ibid., 29.
[102] See music transcription (Figure 3) in Chapter III.
[103] See music transcriptions (Figures 3 and 4) in Chapter III.
[104] Ibid.
[105] See Jazz: A Film by Ken Burns, Episode Three, Our Language [Alexandria, VA], PBS Home Video, 2004.

Indeed, Armstrong was as much aware of the conditions of African Americans as other Renaissance artists. Though Armstrong spent much of his time during the period considered here in Chicago, he could not escape the extent of the nation's social ills, including Ida B. Wells's antilynching campaigns, the growth of Marcus Garvey's Universal Negro Improvement Association, and the popularity of the NAACP. Though Armstrong never expressed an opinion on the matter, the philosophical debate between Du Bois and Garvey was ever-present during the early years of period as the political activism inspired by the post war efforts for liberation were reaching a relative zenith. Harlem was also home to the National Association for the Advancement of Colored People, the Urban League, and the Universal Negro Improvement Association. Each group set forth an agenda and views that spanned a continuum from assimilation and continued efforts toward enfranchisement and constitutional rights to forfeiting said rights and returning to Africa. Their interactions proved as contentious as their theories for black liberation. W. E. B. Du Bois and George Schuyler disagreed with Garvey's theories and motives. Garvey's theories and the existence of the United Negro Improvement Association forced an even more nuanced view of the fate of African-Americans. Both Du Bois and Garvey argued for the liberation of Africa, but the latter's theories of race purity related to the former's heritage made any cooperation between the two in that matter impossible. Importantly, though Garvey's "back to Africa" movement did not come to fruition, the psychological benefit of embracing the African past was evident in much of the period's art.

While in New York, (Armstrong spent much of this time in Chicago) the artist and his group would have performed in or frequented the same venues available to him as Langston Hughes, Countee Cullen, Zora Neal Hurston, and others. He was aware of his popularity as a part of Fletcher Henderson's group as well as his recording of "Black and Blue." Artistically, one of Armstrong's most important accomplishments as an improvisational artist was changing the critical focus of jazz music from the group to the individual soloist while changing the landscape of American vocal and instrumental music.

CHAPTER IV

AGITATE OR CREATE: THE DILEMMA OF BLACK ARTS DURING THE HARLEM RENAISSANCE

Between 1923 and 1930, the flurry of cultural activity primarily in an uptown neighborhood (north of Manhattan) called Harlem, produced numbers of African American artists (literary, performing, and visual) who took advantage of the freedom to create instinctively and market their creations. Simultaneously, the region attracted a variety of African American social and political organizations inspired by a spirit of activism. In separate camps, the groups argued for the enactment of antilynching laws, enforcement of constitutionally guaranteed civil rights, fair housing, and in the latter's case, mass migration to the continent of Africa. Indeed, the assemblage of so many artists and political groups was not a serendipitous event. Armstrong commented, "It (Harlem) had no-good floaters from all over the country, and it had thousands and thousands of good, hard working colored people, and on top of that the most brilliant and talented musicians and actors and poets and artists of our race, mixing there together-they had come from everywhere to Harlem."[106] The area attracted Black American literary, visual, and performing artists because

---

[106] Louis Armstrong, *Armstrong: Swing That Music*, (New York: Da Capo Press, 1936) 81.

of an atmosphere that encouraged and rewarded creativity and artistic expression. According to Armstrong:

> There was Charles Gilpin the great actor in *Emperor Jones*, and Florence Mills, both dead now, and Paul Robeson and Ethel Waters and Bill Robinson and Duke Ellington and Cab Calloway and Chick Webb and James Weldon Johnson, our great poet and those fine people who later went into the cast of *Green Pastures* and carried that beautiful play all over the United States for five years, and many others whom I should mention.[107]

To this end, the cultural movement known as the Harlem Renaissance produced seminal literary, visual, and performing works of art. Contrary to the contemporaneous criticisms of George Schuyler, who questioned the quality and quantity of the art produced during the Harlem Renaissance; others argued an opposing view. The existential question persisted.

What is the purpose and or function of Black arts? Will it serve as a tool to agitate merely exist in prescribed apolitical contexts? W. E. B. Du Bois and others argued that artists should use their creations as propaganda tools, exposing the nation's poor record on race relations. Conversely, Alain Locke cautioned against creating art that did not meet Eurocentric standards. This chapter examines the debate through a textual analysis of W. E. B. Du Bois's 1926 NAACP Convention speech "The Criteria of Negro Art," George Schuyler's essay "The Negro Art-Hokum," Langston Hughes's response "The Negro Artist and the Racial Mountain," and Alain Locke's "The Legacy of Ancestral Arts." The discussion will also examine the specifics of the debate from a performing artist's perspective and in the context of Armstrong's body of work during the period. Precisely, this writer will place Armstrong's recordings "Texas Moaner Blues" (1924), "Black and Blue" (1926), and "West End Blues" (1928) in the context of the debate. The latter

---

[107] Ibid., 81.

will be juxtaposed with Hughes's essay above. This writer's theory is that though Armstrong's contemporaneous influence on the period's visual and literary artists was on the periphery, his performing art significantly changed American blues and jazz music. Armstrong's art seemed to soar above the debate, as it occupied a critical space in American music. Subsequently, his art contributed to the period's political and philosophical debate. Armstrong's art during this period was so significant that it helped to solidify boundaries and cemented philosophical schisms while helping to codify an increasing search for an American music aesthetic. However, the naysayers and the period's detractors could not separate their disdain for reminders of nineteenth-century minstrelsy from the artist's mastery of blues and jazz music.

Armstrong's popularity paralleled the artistic and political activity during the period considered here. His improvisational skills and vocal instincts continued to amaze consumers as he continued an artistic trajectory that began during his developmental years in New Orleans. Indeed, his reputation as a seasoned blues and jazz artist was the result of extraordinary recordings as a leader and as a sideman on many race records. The musical phenomenon did not happen in a vacuum. The period's contributing artists were all products of varying environments that influenced their artistic choices. Armstrong's artistry grew from performing experiences in an American music genre (traditional New Orleans jazz) that emphasized the importance of individualism in the context of an ensemble and with the expectation of a degree of improvisational freedom. His role in changing the art's focus from the importance of the cumulative ensemble production to an emphasis on individual improvisational choices, especially in a blues music context, is arguably his most significant contribution to the genre.[108] In the context of African and African American historical relevance, Armstrong's role as a conduit artist and a cultural agent of change is apparent in his body

---

[108] The consideration here is in the context of Armstrong's artistic experiences with the Joe "King" Oliver Creole Band, the Fletcher Henderson Orchestra, and his own Hot Five and Hot Seven Orchestras.

of work, which spanned approximately forty years following the Harlem Renaissance until he died in 1971.

The years considered here, 1923 to 1930, were arguably one of the most critical eras in the history of African American culture. The fervor of nationalism (partly inspired by the post-World War I global political changes) and the New Negro philosophy helped serve as the impetus for the cultural explosion. It also ignited a debate as to the best paths to gain equal access to the constitutional guarantees, which heretofore were out of reach for people of color and Caucasian women. Black activism sought to make America a true democracy by heroically advocating for freedom for all. In separate camps, George Schuyler, W. E. B. Du Bois, Marcus Garvey, and Ida Barnett Wells all published literature that expressed their multilithic experiences, concerns, and solutions. The subsequent discussion evolved into a philosophical debate as to the role of Black arts.[109] Schuyler openly questioned the quality and quantity of art produced during the Harlem Renaissance. Black artists' dilemma metastasized as supporters simultaneously speculated as to who controls and determines the worth of a body of artistic works. Should Black artists follow their instincts and solely create social realist art exposing the social ills and cultural behaviors inherent in the African American experience, consequently agitating for change? Alternatively, should they seek acceptance from Eurocentric critics and avoid creations based solely upon racial themes?

The artists were not immune to historians Carter G. Woodson's and Arturo Schomburg's research publications, which inspired an increased awareness of African and African American historical contributions to the world. Indeed, their research juxtaposed with the presence and admonitions of Marcus Garvey's "back to Africa" sentiments inspired many African American artists to begin to look to Africa for

---

[109] In addition to the publications previously mentioned by Du Bois and Schuyler, see Marcus Garvey's essay "Africa for Africans," *The Portable Harlem Renaissance Reader*, ed. David Levering Lewis (New York: Penguin Books, 1994), 17 and Ida B. Wells' autobiography, *Crusade for Justice: The Autobiography of Ida Barnett Wells* (Chicago: The University of Chicago Press, 1970), 331–33.

inspiration.[110] Literary artists Langston Hughes, Claude McKay, and Zora Neal Hurston captured the political and social desires, romantic problems, and faiths of their people. Louis Armstrong, Edward "Duke Ellington, and Thomas Wright "Fats" Waller composed, recorded, and played music with racial themes. Similarly, visual artists Aaron Douglas, Romare Bearden, and Richmond Barthe' captured aspects of African American life in various mediums. Not unlike other historical periods, their art was subject to critical review, and some of the era's leading figures weighed in.

Traditionally, artists have grappled with the purpose of their art for as long as the practice has been considered a human phenomenon.[111] Should their art (literary, performance, or visual) be produced for the use of satisfying an aesthetic, or should it expose social conditions and/or advocate a political position? Period literary artist James Weldon Johnson placed the purpose of an artistic body of work in a historical context. "The final measure of the greatness of all peoples is the amount and standard of the literature and art they have produced."[112] Cultural critics and historians with the benefit of hindsight often place works of art in either or both categories. In his landmark research, *How Musical Is Man*, ethnomusicologist John Blacking explained, "What turns one man off may turn another man on, not because of any absolute quality in the music itself but because of what the music has come to mean to him as a member of a particular culture or social group."[113] For

---

[110] Woodson's publication *The Mis-Education of the Negro* (Mineola, NY: Dover Publications, 1933), 122–126 and Schomburg's "The Negro Digs Up His Past," *Voices from the Harlem Renaissance* (New York: Oxford University Press, 1976), 231 are seminal treatises on the methodology used to deliberately eliminate the dissemination of the historical contributions Africa and the West Indies respectively.

[111] Western art-music composers such as J. S. Bach and George Handel are salient examples of performing artists grappling with the purpose of their arts. Specifically, should it adhere to the sacred standards or secular demands.

[112] James Weldon Johnson, *The Book of American Negro Poetry*, First Edition (New York: Harcourt and Brace Co., 1922), vii.

[113] John Blacking, *How Musical Is Man?* (Seattle: The University of Washington Press, 1973), 33.

example, the performance and improvisational art of period soprano saxophonist and clarinetist Sidney Bechet became even more significant after the improvisational explorations of jazz artists Charlie Parker and John Coltrane. The two salient jazz musicians (Parker and Coltrane) contributed to the genre decades later. Often, devotees and consumers of the saxophonists' art sought clues as to the sources of their collective inspirations. Especially when Coltrane explored the possibilities and sonorities of the soprano saxophone. Like Armstrong, they helped to modify the music and inspire imitators throughout the remainder of the twentieth century. Additionally, and pertinent to this research, Armstrong's performing art is not only seminal in the context of the Harlem Renaissance, but it is also salient to the art form as it evolved during the rest of the twentieth century.

It is challenging to discern Armstrong's position on the matter if he had one. Indeed, audience satisfaction was his desired end product. To this end, during his first year of residence in Harlem, he was unhappy with his stint with the Fletcher Henderson Orchestra. Henderson, from Cuthbert, Georgia and trained at Clark College in Atlanta, like many others, shared a kinship with the fellow Southern transplant. By then, having worked, wrote, and arranged for Black Swan records, Henderson was a mainstay on the New York music scene and a contributor to the period's performing art. Armstrong noticed a duality in the group's approach to making music. On the one hand, they dressed impeccably and presented themselves to the public and other artists as some of the period's best jazz and blues musicians. The presentation of his art, which includes its preparation, was of the utmost importance, and Armstrong thought the Henderson group was not as serious about the art as he. Additionally, he was perplexed with the Henderson group's lack of musical curiosity. But he recognized the reputation that preceded his arrival. "I say, Harlem had heard a little about me because many of the New Orleans musicians I had known had drifted up there, they drifted up there, and then, too, they heard about King Oliver's Band in Chicago and had heard his records."[114]

---

[114] Louis Armstrong, *Swing That Music* (New York: Da Capo Press, 1993) 81.

Curiously, period critics chose to marginalize African American artistic creations when they habitually viewed the art in the context of nineteenth-century minstrelsy. Nowhere is the schism more evident than in the theories espoused by Schuyler and Hughes. Schuyler believed that categorizing or labeling art as "Black" reinforced stereotypes that are contrary to the actual African American experience. The period critic loathed plots, texts, and lyrics that celebrated or dignified fictional characters with pernicious behaviors. He surmised, "Because a few writers with a paucity of themes have seized upon imbecilities the Negro rustics and clowns and palmed them off as authentic and characteristic Aframerican behavior, the common notation that the Black American is so 'different' from his white neighbor has gained currency."[115] Hughes on the other hand, advocated for the creation of Black art, propagandized or not. "Let the blare of Negro jazz bands and the bellowing of Bessie Smith singing the Blues penetrate the closed ears of the colored near-intellectuals until they listen and perhaps understand."[116] The Black-owned and operated Pace Phonograph Company did not escape the dilemma. Under the Black Swan record label, the recording company was, according to researcher and Du Bois biographer, David Levering Lewis, "intended to have class and reflect the credit of the race." Lewis further opined, "Moreover, the board of directors was increasingly uneasy about blues recordings."[117]

In this context, blues music's exportation to northern urban areas paved the way for an appropriation of folk caricatures adopted by the lucrative music publishing endeavor called Tin Pan Alley music.[118] The American popular music genre preceded the Harlem Renaissance by

---

[115] George Schuyler, "The Negro-Art Hokum," 1926.
[116] Langston Hughes, "The Negro Artist and the Racial Mountain," 1926
[117] David Levering Lewis, *When Harlem Was In Vogue*, 175
[118] *Tin Pan Alley* is the label given to the canon of songs marketed to blues and jazz music consumers. The songs were written primarily by White American composers during the period considered here. George Gershwin's *Porgy and Bess* is an example of writers and composers that are outside of the culture but consider themselves familiar enough with Black life to produce works of art based on the African American culture.

approximately three decades. Subsequently, while Black American folk music and the Tin Pan Alley recreations were saturating the market during the period considered here, the debate regarding art's purpose reached a relative zenith during the third decade of the twentieth century, and the crux of the discussion was the role and/or use of the era's art.

W. E. B. Du Bois and Alain Locke were at the center of the 'artistic purpose' discussion and ensuing schism. They helped frame the disagreement. Du Bois thought that African American artists should use their mediums as propaganda tools to better the race.[119] Writer and critic Alain Locke, on the other hand, felt that artists needed to create a body of work motivated by the "art for art's sake" mantra.[120] Locke believed that Black artists needed to aspire and reach the critical acceptance of their white counterparts and critics. They had to decide whether to continue to depict African American life in its varied and multidimensional references and risk losing acceptance from and favorable reviews from critics using a Eurocentric barometer. Two decades earlier, Du Bois was sure that just as Paul Lawrence Dunbar, Black writers should use their mediums in whatever contextual vernacular to tell of their people's life truthfully in America.[121] Du Bois also took into consideration the importance of African American music regarding America's contribution to the world. Du Bois opined, "And so by fateful chance the Negro folk song—the rhythmic cry of the slave—stands today not simply as the sole American music but the most beautiful expression of human spirit born this side the seas."[122] He was also concerned with the extent to which white benefactors were influencing artistic decisions. Implicit in Du Bois's concerns was the question as to who decides what qualifies as African American art. He recognized that

---

[119] See Du Bois's speech to the 1926 NAACP Convention, titled "The Criteria of Negro Art," *Crisis Magazine* (October 1926): 10–11.

[120] "Art for art's sake" is a euphemism often used to describe art created with Western or European barometers and no political or social agenda.

[121] See Du Bois's speech, "The Criteria of Negro Art."

[122] W. E. B. Du Bois, *The Souls of Black Folk* (New York: Barnes & Noble Classics, 2005), 251.

critics of the period's art ignored the fact that, like other cultures, the artistic creations of a group rise from self-conscious, aggrandizing, and scholarly efforts. To this end, there is a risk of losing artistic autonomy when artists seek to win approval from those who have a monopoly on the definition of scholarship, art, and culture. David Levering Lewis commented, "But white capital and influence was crucial, and white presence, at least in the early years, hovered over the New Negro world of art and literature like a benevolent censor, politely but pervasively setting the outer limits of its creative boundaries."[123] Thus the dilemma for Black artists was evident. To what degree should well-meaning white benefactors influence their art?

The charitable interest in Black artists came primarily from supporters in two camps. One group was fascinated with African American life from a cultural primitivism perspective. According to Lewis, they were seeking to satisfy a "need for personal nourishment and to confirm their vision of cultural salvation coming from margins of the civilization."[124] The other group perceived sexual themes in the context of Sigmund Freud's theories (published during the second decade of the twentieth century) of sexual repression inspired others.

According to evolutionary psychologist Geoffrey Miller, Freud believed that "human artistic display results from the sublimation of excess sexual energy."[125] White consumers saw (often with envy) Black American cultural behaviors, particularly those associated with music in Harlem, as an outgrowth of the "noble savage" phenomenon. The label suggests that Blacks have a propensity to shed sexual repressions and are free of inhibitions and act upon sexual urge through their performing arts, blues and jazz music.[126] In this Freudian context,

---

[123] David Levering Lewis, *When Harlem Was in Vogue* (New York: Penguin Books, 1997), 98.

[124] Ibid., 99.

[125] Geoffrey Miller, *The Mating Mind* (New York, Anchor Books, 2001) 50.

[126] "Noble savage" is a term used by sociologists and anthropologists to describe behaviors generally present in non-Western groups who were otherwise believed to be outside of the norm or ill-advised in a Eurocentric setting, but a part of the more or folkway of the group considered here.

outsiders erroneously believe the lack of assimilation into American culture allows for a degree of promiscuity, or at the very least, an insinuation of sexual freedom. Many of the same outsiders, mainly white consumers, were willing to partake in the sexually tinged mores and folkways apparent in African American performing art on display nightly in Harlem. Albert Murray contextualized the ill-conceived propensity to categorize the art:

> As downright aphrodisiac as blues music so often becomes, however, and as notorious for violence as the reputation of the blues-oriented dance-hall records has been over the years, blues-idiom merriment is not marked either by the sensual abandonment of the voodoo orgy or by the ecstatic trance of a religious possession. One of its most distinctive features, conversely is its unique combination of spontaneity, improvisation, and control.[127]

In this context, Du Bois was concerned with the enormity and consistency of many white patrons' generosities, particularly the possibility of ulterior motives. Levering Lewis believed that Du Bois had stopped just short of seeing a white conspiracy behind the Renaissance. However, he underscored the apparent truth that there was "a surprising number of white people who are getting great satisfaction out of these younger Negro writers. Because they think it is going to stop the Negro question."[128] Du Bois's position on the matter was clear. He welcomed philanthropic capital, even sought it for the National Association for the Advancement of Colored People but cautioned artists to maintain artistic autonomy and advocate for racial equality.

The opposing view to Du Bois's theories came from fellow Harvard alum, cultural critic, and author of the publication *The New Negro*, Alain Locke. Importantly, Locke was responsible for many of the

---

[127] Albert Murray, *Stomping The Blues* (New York: Da Capo Press, 1976) 50.
[128] David Levering Lewis, *W. E. B. Dubois: The Fight for Equality and the American Century 1919–1963* (New York: Henry Holt & Co., 2000), 181.

introductions of period literary and visual artists to willing benefactors. He believed that if artists solely use areas of black life and experiences as the single theme for their art, they will affirm the critics' argument that their body of work lacks artistic worth, is monotonous, and mostly subpar. However, Locke's position seems to come from contrary points of view. His bifurcated view simultaneously advocated the Eurocentric barometer to African American art as he believed visual artists should (just as European artists Matisse and Picasso) look to the centuries-old artistic practices of their West African counterparts.[129] Expressly, Locke acknowledged the contributions of the continent's ancient visual art practices to early twentieth-century Western culture by endorsing Matisse's and Picasso's West African-inspired creations. On the other hand, he believed that singularly focused African American visual art was lacking diversity despite their indebtedness to West African practices. Locke opined, "The characteristic African art expressions are rigid, controlled, disciplined, abstract, heavily conventionalized; those of the Aframerican [sic]—free, exuberant, emotional, sentimental and human. Only by misinterpretation of the African spirit, can one claim any emotional kinship between them—for the spirit of African expression, by and large, is disciplined, sophisticated, and fatalistic. The emotional temper of the American Negro is exactly the opposite."[130]

Contrary to Du Bois, Locke believed that Harlem Renaissance visual artists should adopt the European model of development while lamenting the body of non-European Western art. "While American art including the work of our own Negro artists, has produced nothing above the level of the genre study or more penetrating than a Nordicized transcription, European art has gone on experimenting until the technique of the Negro subject has reached the dignity and skill of virtuoso treatment and a distinctive style." Locke explained, "The work of these European artists should even now be inspiration and guideposts of a younger school of American Negro artists. They have too long been

---

[129] See Alain Locke's essay, "The Legacy of Ancestral Arts," *The New Negro*, ed. Alain Locke (New York: Atheneum Publishers, 1925), 254–67.

[130] Locke, "Art or Propaganda," *Harlem* (November 1928): 256.

victims of the academy tradition and shared the conventional blindness of the Caucasian eye with respect to the racial material at their immediate disposal. Thus, there have been notably successful Negro artists, but no development of a school of Negro art."[131] Subsequently, the dilemma Black visual, literary, and performing artists faced was to use their art to agitate or follow creative instincts that may lead to nonracial or general themes. Some of the period's visual artists acquiesced to the Du Bois school of thought and produced works that were in the social realism idiom. In various mediums, visual artists Aaron Douglas, Romare Bearden, and Archibald Motley produced works that depicted Black life in Harlem indicative of Du Bois's admonitions. Douglas biographer Amy Helene Kirsche believed Harlem's black leaders were aware of the cultural atmosphere.[132] "Harlem's new intellectual class self-consciously believed that they were witnessing a renaissance, or rebirth, of African American culture. Poetry, prose, the visual arts, theater, dance, and music were all integral to their vision of rebirth."[133] Indeed, the "intellectual class" Kirsche referred to had to choose whether to accept African American arts (literary, visual, and performance) as indicators of progress and proof of humanity deserving of America's constitutional promises imacy of the period's art. They believed the period was more a product of some philanthropists' fantasies than an accurate account of the cultural era."[134] Succinctly, to achieve an accurate analysis of the debate, one must view the creative choices expressed by the artists in the context of the diverse realities that are black life in America. According to Houston Baker Jr., it was "difficult to conceive of the horribleness of the American scene for black

Aaron Douglas
(Archives, Fisk University)

---

[131] Ibid.

[132] Locke, "The Legacy of the Ancestral Arts," 256.

[133] Amy Helene Kirsche, *Aaron Douglas: Art, Race, and the Harlem Renaissance* (Jackson: University Press of Mississippi, 1995), 33.

[134] David Levering Lewis discusses the continuum in detail in *When Harlem Was in Vogue*.

people during the era that Locke produced his classic collection (*The New Negro*)."¹³⁵ Indeed, regarding their livelihood, most of the artists depended on charitable gifts. To Baker's point, Locke suggested that solely using aspects of African American life and experiences under Jim Crow South and the oppressive North, affirms to critics that there is a lack of artistic talent, and such a body of work would be monotonous as well as subpar.

Interestingly, blues and jazz music satisfied Locke's desire to find a Black American art that meets the litmus test of the dominant culture. The performing art (already more than three decades old) was becoming two of America's most famous musical idioms. By 1925, blues music had become a permanent fixture in American culture with many of its salient progenitors such as Bessie Smith, Ethel Waters, and Louis Armstrong (periodically) living in the Harlem community. Consumers purchased their recordings by the thousands, and the artists consistently sold-out live performances. The phenomenon was indicative of the performing art's popularity among America's black and white citizens. Paradoxically, Caucasian-American consumers' aesthetic yearnings were satisfied after experiencing the music. Indeed, the salient dual-modality served as the primary aquifer for the performing art's popularity. Black and white or contrary to Kirsche's opinion, reject the arts as detrimental to their desired racial progress. Albert Murray offered this opinion: "Some cultural critics and historians questioned the legit-consumers alike embraced the satisfaction of hearing artistry created on a relatively simplistic music form (chiefly twelve bars or increments), which allowed for improvisation, accompanied or not. Blues music also functioned as a liberating aesthetic for African Americans.

Explicitly, the performing artists musically acknowledged particular aspects of everyday life (failed romance, racial oppression, the death of a loved one, or their mortality) that were responsible for much of an individual's (consumer) emotional pain.¹³⁶ Like their enslaved ancestors'

---

¹³⁵ Houston A. Baker Jr., *Modernism and the Harlem Renaissance*, 76.

¹³⁶ The reader is encouraged to investigate the lyrics or texts of a cross-section of early blues songs. W. C. Handy's *St. Louis Blues*, referred to in Chapter V, is a salient example of early blues music.

repeated singing and hearing of spirituals, blues music-makers and consumers received a melancholy-relief from the performing art. Psychologically, the first step to liberation from life's troubling nuances is to recognize and acknowledge their source(s). This writer will explore this aspect of blues music in more detail in Chapter V.

The performing art considered here, as all the other period arts, did not exist in a vacuum. Many of the era's literary artists did not escape the performing art's African American aesthetic tentacles as writers assumed the Du Bois mantel and created works that exposed America's societal ills. Writers, Claude McKay, Sterling Brown, and Langston Hughes (whom Locke considered indicative of *The New Negro*) consistently wrote literary works with blues music as its central theme. Harlem Renaissance theorist and historian Nathan Irving Huggins noted the genre's impact upon Langston Hughes. Huggins explained, "Langston Hughes conceived of poetry as the music of the common people's language, captured and tied to the images in their minds."[137] Hughes explained, "Many of my early poems were efforts to touch the dignity of the common man's life."[138] David Levering Lewis summarized many of the artists' creative dilemmas. Specifically, their artistic choices when juxtaposed with the politics and aesthetics of the time: "In their contempt for propagandist literature and disdain for literary politics, and their dogged struggles simply to be themselves, they tested the outermost limits of what was possible for people of African ancestry dedicated to the creative life. Still—for paradox was the essence of their being—an objective survey reveals that McKay played literary politics shamelessly and Toomer became a rigid propagandist."[139] Hughes's, McKay's, and Toomer's literary choices serve as hallmark examples of the period's canon. Each faced the dilemma of determining their artistic choices dissimilarly, while collectively embracing the performing arts' impact on the period.

---

[137] Nathan Irvin Huggins, *Harlem Renaissance* (New York: Oxford University Press, 2007), 78.
[138] Ibid., 78.
[139] Lewis, *When Harlem Was in Vogue*, 50.

In the context of the "agitate or create" debate, Langston Hughes's belief that the African American artist should remain faithful to his or her passions was evident. Particularly when they are expressing the experiences of Black life in America. In 1926, Hughes argued this point in "The Negro Artist and the Racial Mountain." He believed that regardless of audience or patron demands, Black artists should adhere to their creative instincts, particularly when expressing social injustices. Hughes noted the dubious decision Black artists must make concerning their creative impulses as well as the consequences of those choices. He believed that if the Eurocentric model is the standard of the arts, then African American artists are consequently forced to choose whether or not to create reflections of their community's culture with depictions and/or texts that are contrary to American ideals. Furthermore, the artists must then disregard the African American experience (to satisfy a false premise) while trying to subscribe to the expectations of some consumers and cultural critics.[140] One of the outcomes of Black artists ignoring the realities of Black American experiences in a dominant culture that prefers them to portray African American life and history as frivolous, noncontributing, unworthy, inferior, and non-achieving, is cultural suicide.

Schuyler derided Locke, Du Bois, and others for promulgating and promoting the presence of Black American art. Schuyler's position is, such as it exists, that African American art is subpar and inconsequential. Precisely, he believed that any Black literary and visual arts were mere imitations of European models, values, standards, and barometers. According to Schuyler, "As was for the literature, painting and sculpture of Aframericans—such as there is—it is identical in kind with the kind of literature, painting, and sculpture of white Americans: that is, it shows more or less evidence of European influence."[141] The latter is contrary to the very foundation (improvisational techniques) of American jazz and blues music. It is a critic's prerogative to argue for the placement of Black art in Eurocentric parameters. Conversely,

---

[140] George Schuyler's views in his essay, "The Negro Art-Hokum," is an example of this.
[141] George Schuyler, "The Negro-Art Hokum," 310.

blues and jazz music are intrinsic to the American music canon. They are two of the nation's indigenous performing art canons. Though they were decades old, their productions during the decade after World War I, came amid an American nationalistic search. Consequently, the genres were both celebrated and loathed in the context of political and philosophical opinions of individuals searching for paths to civil liberties in the twentieth century.

Hughes also expressed dismay with another outgrowth of the Black artistic dilemma. Specifically, the strange behavior among many Blacks who did not accept or acknowledge Black art until their Eurocentric counterparts confirmed its validity. Hughes said, "For racial culture the home of a self-styled 'high-class' Negro has nothing better to offer. Instead there will perhaps be more aping of things white than in a less cultured or less wealthy home."[142] Seven years later, historian Carter G. Woodson discussed the phenomena and argued for multiculturalism in the arts:

> These "highly educated" Negroes, however, fail to see that it is not the Negro that takes position. The white man forces him to it, and to eradicate himself there from, the Negro leader must so deal with the situation as to develop in the segregated group the power with which they can elevate themselves. The differentness of races, moreover, is no evidence of superiority or inferiority. This merely indicates that each race has certain gifts which the other does not possess. It is by the development of these gifts that every race must justify its right to exist.[143]

The question then is who sets the standards and how appropriate is it to assign the European model to African American arts? On the other hand, Du Bois and Locke both advocated for excellence and high standards in Black arts. However, Locke believed that while artists

---

[142] Hughes, "The Negro Artist and the Racial Mountain," 306.
[143] Woodson, *The Mis-Education of the Negro*, 5.

should resist the temptation to please patrons solely, they should seek to attain Western standards. "Negro things may reasonably be a fad for others; for us they must be a religion. Beauty, however, is its best priest and psalms will be more effective sermons."[144] Conversely, Du Bois was concerned with artistic control. "We want Negro writers to produce beautiful things but we stress the things."[145]

Philosophical conflicts were never more apparent than when poet Claude McKay insisted on using race and race-pride as his themes when he penned a protest poem titled "White House." Much to the poet's chagrin, Locke changed the title of McKay's poem to "White Houses" before publishing the work in the *Survey Graphic* Magazine. The periodical was a significant conduit for aesthetic and political theories considered as *New Negro* sentiments. He (Locke) believed propagandized art would receive harsh treatment, and Black literary artists who are representative of the New Negro, such as McKay, Hughes, and Sterling Brown would not earn the desired critical endorsement. Additionally, naysayers would see the Black experience in a single context, consequently relegating their works as merely parochial. In 1934 Harlem Renaissance visual artist Romare Bearden serendipitously contributed to the discussion from an insider's point of view: "This of course will impress the initiated, who through some feeling of inferiority toward their own subject matter, only require that a work of art have some sort of foreign stamp of to make it acceptable."[146] Cultural critic and Harlem Renaissance scholar Houston Baker Jr. argued: "I came to realize that of what passes for self-consciously 'scholarly' effort on the part of black men and women in the United States is often production, self-consciously oriented to win approval from those who have a monopoly on definitions of scholarship."[147] To this end, Hughes understood the importance of his and others' artistic choices: "An artist must be free to choose what he does, certainly, but he must also never be

---

[144] Locke, "Art or Propaganda," 219.
[145] W. E. B. Du Bois, "Criteria of Negro Art," *Crisis Magazine* (October 1926): 295.
[146] Romare Bearden, "The Negro Artist and Modern Art," *Opportunity* (December 1934): 37.
[147] Ibid., xvii.

afraid to do what he might choose."[148] The schism is apparent, as many of the literary artists embraced Du Bois's and Hughes's admonitions and produced works reflecting the black experience in America.

Much of the subject matter in the genre considered here was contrary to Locke's wishes. They varied in subject matter from social realism, romance, to terrorism. The works range from *Cane* by Jean Toomer, Jessie Redmond Fauset's "La Vie C'est La Vie," and the politically charged poems "White House," "If We Must Die," and "Harlem Dancer" by Claude McKay. "Yet Do I Marvel" by Countee Cullen is one of the period's seminal works. The poem is a thoughtful introspective of his curiosity as to why he had literary and creative instincts bestowed upon him through divine ordination, juxtaposed with an existence under an oppressive regime in the United States.[149] Additionally, James Weldon Johnson's 1927 collection of seven sermons titled *God's Trombones* is a creative and successful attempt to place the role of the Black preacher in the context of poetry.[150]

Curiosity inspired period novelist, researcher, and folklorist Zora Neal Hurston explored Southern African American culture as an insider having grown up in the region. One cannot overstate Hurston's contributions to the legacy of the period's literary and performing arts.

Indeed, Hurston gives readers a glimpse of the music and folklife for many Blacks who chose not to migrate north. Their decision not to leave the South allowed Hurston, Alan Lomax, and other musicologists to experience blues music, and in Hurston's case, folktales in their rural settings. Hurston's and Lomax's efforts exposed the fact that many consumers held a fascination and often romanticized about the social conditions that produced blues music. Many believed they were getting an authentic glimpse of the art reproduced in or from (in the case of live performances) Southern United States settings, notwithstanding their existence in oppression, disenfranchisement, bigotry, and the perpetual threat of terrorism. In this writer's opinion, one of the keys to the music's

---

[148] Langston Hughes, "The Negro Artist and the Racial Mountain," 95.

[149] The last line on Countee Cullen's poem, "Yet Do I Marvel," "To make a poet black, and bid him sing" is indicative of the poet's torment.

[150] James Weldon Johnson, *God's Trombones* (New York: Viking Press, 1927).

popularity is that, in most instances, the performing art melodically identified one's ills and offered solutions. This problem-solution musical paradigm is one of the factors that induced an individual and collective optimism that inspired consumers to gravitate to the art. The period's artists, philosophers, politicians, and theorists recognized the importance of the period's arts, particularly their impact on the lives of consumers. However, the schism was pervasive; and the question seemed perpetual, what is the purpose of African American art?

Pertinent to the discussion here, documenting folk art in Albert Murray's context (see citation in Chapter One) was equally important and challenging, particularly when one considers from which perspective (insider or outsider) will such research occupy. In 1935, from an insider's point of view, Hurston documented and published a collection of folk tales and songs she heard while traveling in the South, titled *Mules and Men*. The publication includes work songs, prison-field hollers, and the early blues music prevalent before the great migration. Hurston's mentor, noted anthropologist and Barnard College professor Franz Boaz, recognized Hurston's anthropological instincts and encouraged her to act on the curiosity regarding African American folklore. Hurston's interest began as a child growing up in the South and blossomed while attending Howard University. Interestingly, Hurston's academic training initially inspired an outsider approach to her research. However, she was not satisfied with the results and discussed her dilemma in her autobiography:

> The glamour of Barnard College was still upon me. I dwelt in marble halls. I knew where the material was all right. But, I went about asking, in carefully Barnadese, "Pardon me, but do you know any folk tales or folk songs?" The men and women who had whole treasuries of material just seeping through their pores, looked at me and shook their heads.[151]

---

[151] Zora Neal Hurston, *Dust Tracks on a Road* (New York: Harper Collins Publishers, 1942), 144–5.

By 1926, nine years before *Mules and Men*, the debate was reaching a zenith as Du Bois's "The Criteria of Negro Art," speech was indicative of how divisive the subject was. The fact that he chose to discuss the impact and possibilities of using the arts as an exposé on the struggles of African Americans is indicative of his recognition and validation of the quality and validity of the period's arts. Du Bois argued for the necessity of black artists to aspire beyond the Eurocentric model of pulchritude and success. He thought that African American artists should seek to create their genuineness with regards to their existence, which would serve as a conduit for liberty. Du Bois stated his position,

> The apostle of Beauty thus becomes the apostle of Truth and Right not by choice but inner and outer compulsion. Free he is but his freedom is never bounded by Truth and Justice, and slavery only dogs him when he is denied the right to tell the Truth or recognize an ideal of justice. Thus art is propaganda and ever must be, despite the wailing of the purists. I stand in utter shamelessness and say that whatever art I have for writing has been used always for propaganda for gaining the right of black folk to love and enjoy. I do not care a damn for any art that is not used for propaganda. But I do care when propaganda is confined to one side while the other is stripped and silent.[152]

Deeper still, Du Bois believed that the striving for acceptance model is a fruitless endeavor when the artist's creations are contrary to their instincts, subsequently producing art as an outsider. It is not clear if the period's performing arts were in the context of his theory. However, by 1926, blues and jazz music were integral to the era's cultural experience, and Louis Armstrong's performing artistry was fueling the genres' aesthetic importance. The evidence lies in the rising sales of blues

---

[152] Ibid., 296.

recordings, cultural indicators as noted in the previous chapter, Du Bois and other period contributors could not escape.

Louis Armstrong's impact on the genre's popularity is more than an unintended consequence. While Hughes, Sterling Brown, Aaron Douglas, and others created important visual and literary works with blues music (and the associated cultural behaviors) as a theme Armstrong was simultaneously one of blues music's chief contributors. The genre was on a trajectory that paralleled the performing art's approbation and popularity in American culture. Subsequently, the nation's major recording companies created "race record" divisions as a marketing strategy to take advantage of the performing art's popularity primarily in the black community. Eileen Southern discussed OKeh Recording Company's 1921 reaction to the consumer demand for Mamie Smith's recordings, "Crazy Blues" and "It's Right Here for You": "The demand for this record in black communities was so enormous that OKeh realized for the first time the vast potential market among blacks for blues and blues-jazz."[153] Southern expounded further:

> The race record industry was off with a bang! Other companies soon pushed into the market: Columbia, during the years 1923-33, with its 14000D series featuring stars such as Bessie Smith, Ethel Waters, and Clara Smith; Paramount (1922-32) with its 12000 series, called "Popular Race Records," and such singers as Alberta Hunter, Ida Cox, Charley Patton, and "Blind" Lemon Jefferson.[154]

For his part, Armstrong recorded hundreds of blues songs as a bandleader with his Hot Five and Hot Seven groups while recording 114 times as a sideman (accompanist) to other blues artists which makes him essential in the context of the genre's popularity with Black and white consumers.[155] His artistic activity, which included live performances,

---

[153] Eileen Southern, *The Music of Black Americans*, 370.
[154] Ibid., 370
[155] See the detailed discographies (Appendices A and B).

makes him one of the music's chief progenitors. The activity included accompanying some of the genre's most salient vocalists, Ma Rainey, Bessie Smith, and Mamie Smith. Researcher Gilbert M. Erskine surmised: "It is no secret that Louis Armstrong did some of his best playing accompanying singers on their recordings."[156] More importantly, in almost every studio setting, period performing artists were expressing through blues music, the social indicators predominant in African American life. They often included a failed romance ("St. Louis Blues"), lost or no employment ("Dark Was the Night"), contemplating death and the afterlife ("See That My Grave Is Kept Clean"), the victim of racially motivated terrorism and other social injustices ("Jim Crow Blues").

Artistically, Armstrong took advantage of opportunities to express cultural pride by evoking improvisations and vocal techniques that, while remaining faithful to the context of the art considered here (blues and jazz music), was subconsciously transforming the American music canon. Though some of his improvisational choices were repeated and routine, his initial improvisational instincts were born out of experiences a decade earlier in New Orleans.

In that setting, just as in the studios of OKeh and Columbia Recording Companies, improvisational art created in the moment was always in the context of specific roles, all dependent upon immediate production. Armstrong's creativity and subsequent impact alluded to earlier are apparent in his 1928 rendition of Joe "King" Oliver's "West End Blues." The recording is a masterful reflection from an artist/revolutionary whose genius allows him to make those who would otherwise subject him to the ravages of Jim Crow laws and bigotry comfortable while simultaneously making an artistic and political statement. Transforming a culture through music can be revolutionary. Significantly, Armstrong's improvisational choices in "West End Blues" were executed with the confidence of a revolutionary determined to make an artistic statement. This fact is when the listener juxtaposes

---

[156] Gilbert M. Erskine, "'Countin' The Blues: A Survey of the Recordings of Louis Armstrong Accompanying Singers in the 1920s," *The Second Line* (Spring, 1976): 10.

Armstrong's improvised solo in the context of the blues form with his introductory fanfare. The two artistic choices (on the same recording) are musically on opposite ends of a continuum. The landmark session took place on the heels of Schuyler and Hughes's seminal publications two years earlier. In separate mediums, Armstrong and Hughes are making the same argument.

An analysis of Armstrong's opening fanfare (see Figure 3) reveals not only the artist's command of the art, but also a codifying of (through music) Hughes's position in "The Negro Artist and the Racial Mountain." The point here is that Armstrong juxtaposed the period's most prominent performing art (African American folk music) with an improvised European (Western) classical trumpet fanfare. The result was a seminal moment in the history of American music. Indeed, Armstrong's introduction to "West End Blues" is reflective of one of Hughes's points, "when he chooses to touch on the relations between Negroes and whites in this country with their many overtones and undertones surely, and especially for literature and the drama, there is an inexhaustible supply of themes at hand."[157]

In this context, Armstrong's rendition of "West End Blues" is an example of a performing art produced from the perspective of an agent of change. Literary critic Houston Baker Jr. noted the propensity of such change agents to deconstruct or arrange the deformation of masks as a tool for liberation. In this context, Armstrong's artistry of juxtaposing Western art music with blues music was a display, or as Baker Jr. wrote a "coding of African, tribal, or social sounds as active, outgoing resistance and response to oppressive ignorance and silencing."[158] Some scholars argue that a common characteristic among all artists is a propensity to question their paths regarding the adherence to

Louis Armstrong
(Louis Armstrong House and Museum)

---

[157] Hughes, "The Negro Artist and the Racial Mountain," 307.
[158] Houston Baker Jr., *Blues, Ideology and Afro-American Literature: A Vernacular Theory*, 104.

preset standards or following creative urges. In this context, a more in-depth analysis of Armstrong's choices here and the Hughes reveals a performing artist unknowingly (as there is no evidence of Armstrong reading Hughes's essay) embracing the cultural uniqueness born out of blues music.

The beginning of Armstrong's opening fanfare was typical of much of the Western music literature written for the trumpet (see Figure 3). Atypical, however, was Armstrong's immediate departure (measure six) to the blues music idiom. At that point in the introduction, the listener will hear the New Orleans blues music approach from Armstrong. Hughes unwittingly discussed Armstrong's and his influences: "But then there are the low-down folks, the so-called common element, and they are the majority—may the Lord be praised!" theories expressed by are not too important to themselves or community, or too well fed, or too learned to watch the lazy world go round."[159]

Figure 3. Louis Armstrong's opening fanfare to "West End Blues"

Hughes asserted further, "They furnish a wealth of colorful distinctive material for any artist because they still hold their own individuality in the face of American standardizations."[160] Armstrong's rendition of West End Blues codifies Hughes's admonitions. Musically, he instinctively embraces the cultural uniqueness of his life in New Orleans. Indeed, his childhood neighborhood was called the "Battlefield"

---

[159] Hughes, "The Negro Artist and the Racial Mountain," 306.
[160] Ibid.

because of the profusion of violent crimes present in most economically-depressed communities[161] in America. Many of the people familiar to young Armstrong would fit into Hughes's "low-down people" category. By 1928, the year he recorded West End Blues, Armstrong was aware that the "Battlefield" and other neighborhoods in New Orleans had to endure a perpetually depressed economy, which played a role in fostering pernicious characters that took advantage of criminal opportunities.

In "West End Blues," Armstrong immediately and masterfully gives the listener a glimpse of the Western music tradition of using trumpet fanfares to generate anticipation of an impending event.[162] Hughes endorsed such artistic choices (in this case, Armstrong's decision to implement a blues descent) and encouraged Black artists to embrace their African American instincts. To this end, in "West End Blues," Armstrong successfully navigated (in the context of twelve-bar blues choruses) a call-response vocalese approach and an improvised trumpet solo reminiscent of his earlier art in "Heebie Jeebies." Certainly, the fanfare or opening musical statement suggested anything but the slow melancholy nature of his version of the song.[163] Hughes further postulates that when African Americans embrace the Eurocentric model or Western art as the standard, a degree of self-hate arises, especially when all art has to meet such standards. According to Hughes, "The whisper of 'I want to be white' runs through their minds."[164] When the essay's antagonist and Armstrong are juxtaposed, Hughes's next point is ironic. "One sees immediately how difficult it would be for an artist born in such a home to interest himself in interpreting the beauty of his own people. He is never taught to see that beauty. He is taught rather not to see it, or if he does, to be ashamed of it when it is not to Caucasian patterns."[165] Conversely, Armstrong's innate ability to see beauty even in some of the worst aspects

---

[161] Armstrong, *Satchmo*, 73–88.

[162] The reader should note that there is an error on beat four of the first measure. It should be G#.

[163] In this context, a chorus is a twelve-bar or measured sequence repeated with a different text.

[164] Ibid.

[165] Ibid., 307.

of life in New Orleans during his childhood and adolescence helped him codify and exemplify Hughes's theory.[166] Indeed, the early jazz-music pioneers, especially Joe "King" Oliver, were in Armstrong's orbit, and they played a significant role in his cultural insights.

Since the instrument's inclusion in Western classical music, it has not been uncommon for composers to use trumpet fanfares to set an ambiance in music.[167] Two of jazz music's earliest pioneers, Buddy Bolden and trombonist Kid Ory, used a similar approach (fanfares) to announce events or manipulate crowds on many occasions in New Orleans. Musician Johnny St. Cyr described Bolden's fanfare explorations in a 1962 letter to researcher Donald Marquis. "Bolden had a certain theme he would insert into everything he played."[168] Others referred to Bolden's fanfare as "calling his children home." Armstrong recalled trombonist Kid Ory's signature theme used to affirm a musical triumph often against a rival group. "Kid Ory's Band would cut all the Bands, during his tailgate advertising. The crowd would Roar and Applaud when Kid Ory would blow a few bars on his trombone, as his wagon was leaving, a tuned called 'Kiss My Ass.'"[169] Armstrong experienced first-hand the musical approach and the cultural behaviors associated with them.

His experiences are evident in his opening fanfare as he initially (the first measure) adopted the same approach in "West End Blues." Bolden's, Ory's, and others' performing arts were steeped in his memory as Armstrong recalled the associated African American mores and folkways of New Orleans and listening to his mentor. Particularly, participating in a communal cultural behavior called the *second line*. The behavior consisted of collectively following the movement of a parading band while executing individualistic dances reminiscent of

---

[166] Thomas Brothers' *Louis Armstrong's New Orleans* gives the reader an in-depth view of Armstrong's childhood community.
[167] The reader is encouraged to hear various examples of the use of the trumpet in Western art-music. An example of this practice can be heard in Ludwig Van Beethoven's *Lenoir Overture*.
[168] Letter to Donald Marquis, 1962.
[169] Armstrong, *In His Own Words, Selected Writings*, (New York, Oxford University Press, 1999) 28.

the enslaved in Congo Square. Armstrong described the importance of participating in such events and the opportunities to see musicians, including his idol, while still learning the trumpet. "I still stayed with the Karnofskys, playing around with my horn in my spare time. And second line in the bands and Funerals, following behind my *idol* Joe Oliver when and wherever he played. Whether it was a parade—Funeral or *Funky Butt Hall*."[170] A more detailed analysis of the introduction to "West End Blues" reveals Armstrong's salient musical instincts. Precisely, after the initial musical ascent in Western art-music fashion, his cascading blues-tinged descent culminated with a definitive augmented conclusion, played as if repeating the musical motif would ensure that the listener understands and anticipates the art that follows. Armstrong successfully navigated African American folk music (blues) with a European (Western) classical trumpet fanfare. The creation resulted in a seminal moment in the history of American music.[171] Hughes theorized that such artistic choices (such as Armstrong's in "West End Blues" two years later) could potentially achieve acceptance of African American cultural contributions to American culture. Such an end result would satisfy Alain Locke's admonitions.

One should not underestimate the significance of New Orleans as a precursor to the Harlem Renaissance's performing art and, thus, the period's literary and visual arts. There is a correlation between the cultural origins of the region's music, associated cultural behavior, and Hughes's theory. Oliver's composition named for a popular venue in New Orleans that would have been familiar to many of the New Orleans bred musicians who migrated north to Chicago, northeast to Harlem, and west to California during the years before and during the Harlem Renaissance. The cultural interactions at West End took place in the context of the city's ruling class's decision to designate Sundays as the day off. The region's Black musicians took advantage of the designated day of leisure much in the same tradition as the enslaved in Congo Square did some sixty to seventy years earlier on the same day

---

[170] Ibid., 14.
[171] Hughes, "The Negro Artist and the Racial Mountain," 306.

of the week. The city's white and Black population developed a unique folkway. Armstrong biographer Thomas Brothers opined,

> When Protestant Americans began moving to New Orleans in large numbers after the Louisiana Purchase of 1803, they were shocked to discover how the French and Spanish Catholics behaved on Sundays: it was not a day of contemplation and remorse but rather one of gambling, picnicking, dancing, and drinking. (This was precisely how Place Congo had fit into the local scene, as the weekly slave version of Sunday celebration).[172]

Brothers commented further,

> The train delivered them all (musicians and party-goers) to the western end of the line, a spot known simply as "West End" and later immortalized in Armstrong's recording of West End Blues, from 1927. Whites disembarked on one side, blacks on the other. Bands still looking for work that day auditioned on the boardwalk, right at the train stop, trying to catch the attention of disembarking passengers.[173]

Competition and interaction between downtown and uptown bands as well as some white bands bred creativity. Just as Bolden and John Robicheaux competed on Sundays for crowds at adjacent Johnson and Lincoln Parks in the Carrolton section of the city, groups followed suit at the West End gatherings.

The musicians who accompanied Armstrong on "West End Blues" (particularly New Orleans-born drummer Zutty Singleton) understood their role(s). They were aware of jazz pioneers Buddy Bolden's and John Robicheaux's legendary competitions as well as the legacy of his and

---

[172] Thomas Brothers, *Louis Armstrong's New Orleans* (New York, London: W.W. Norton Co. 2006), 223.

[173] Ibid., 223

Armstrong's enslaved fore parents' social behavior in Congo Square. Significantly, New Orleans's, Harlem's, and indeed America's blues and jazz artists interacted with each other, sharing musical ideas while being proud of the music's origins. Brothers also shared his theories about the music's sources and resulting social outcomes: "It has been claimed that cultural innovation often comes from the margins of society. New Orleans had lots of margins, and they were all connected in some slippery way to every other venue along any number of musical social tangents."[174] Subsequently, the artists, including the all-White Original Dixieland Jazz Band (the first group to record), shared their approach to music making to new audiences in America, helping to create an original art form that the nation could boast as its own.

The artistic instincts of Harlem's new creative residents, which included Armstrong, Edward "Duke" Ellington, Fletcher Henderson, Cullen, Hurston, Sterling Brown, Romare Bearden, and Aaron Douglas did not go unnoticed by "New Negro" enthusiast, Locke:

> The migrant masses, shifting from countryside to city, hurdle several generations of experience at a leap, but more important, the same thing happens spiritually in the life-attitudes and self-expression of the young Negro, in his poetry, his art, his education and his new outlook, with the additional advantage, of course, of the poise and greater certainty of knowing what it is all about.[175]

The musician's quest for acceptance by a society that established a physical and cultural boundary between Harlem and Manhattan as well as described the music in such a degrading (in the eyes of the period's naysayers) label as "jungle music" would have inspired Locke to shun any art that adhered to that aesthetics, notwith-standing its popularity. However, by 1926 blues and jazz music was integral to the period's cultural experience, and Louis Armstrong's performing artistry helped

---

[174] Ibid., 224.
[175] Locke, *The New Negro*, 48.

fuel the genre's aesthetic importance. His artistic contributions seem to have soared above the debate while covertly inspiring the literary world, with an individuality apparent in his improvisational choices.[176] This writer explores blues music as a source of inspiration for some of the salient poems written by Langston Hughes and Sterling Brown in the next chapter.

    Succinctly, jazz music served as a conduit for the opportunity for individual expression while creating art instantly, and few mastered it as well as Armstrong during the third decade of the twentieth century. It is not mere happenstance that his rendition of West End Blues rendition of "West End Blues" came during the midst of the Du Bois-Locke-Hughes-Schuyler debate, and blues music was the aquifer for the period's performing art and thus integral to discussions or debates as to the purpose of the validity of said art. More importantly, by 1928, Armstrong was one of the most influential blues artists in America. Although musicologists have recognized the fanfare as a historically significant artistic expression, it has been heard primarily in the context of the American jazz canon as opposed to a "nationalistic" American music canon. Historians Donald D. Megill and Richard S. Demory opined, "Perhaps the most celebrated and thoroughly analyzed record of this period is 'West End Blues,' recorded by Louis Armstrong in June 1928 with the Hot Five. Armstrong begins the Joe 'King' Oliver tune with a trumpet solo that according to many jazz historians redirected the course of jazz."[177] However, Armstrong's improvised solo played after the fanfare is indicative of instinctive artistry bridging Du Bois's and Locke's arguments (see Figure 4).

---

[176] See Figure 1 in Chapter I.
[177] Donald D. Megill, and Richard S. Demory, *Introduction to Jazz History*, (Englewood Cliffs, CA: Prentice-Hall, Inc., 1984) 60.

Figure 4. Louis Armstrong's improvised solo in *West End Blues*

Further analysis of "West End Blues" shows that Armstrong's opening fanfare cleverly establishes a sense of anticipation that gives no hint of the rendition's dirge-like setting. The accompanying musicians on the recording are pianist Earl "Fatha" Hines, trombonist Fred Robinson, clarinetist Jimmy Strong, Mancy Carr on banjo, and Zutty Singleton on drums.[178] They were all steeped in the blues tradition as the session's leader, Armstrong embraced the West African and African American music tradition of call response.[179] Specifically, Armstrong's role after the introduction became a supportive one. The first chorus begins with Strong's melodic statement and Armstrong's vocal imitation. The reader may note (the non-musician will hear) the analysis of this musical approach and the resulting polyphony of the wind instruments in a traditional New Orleans brass band explored earlier in "Texas Moaner Blues" (see Figure 2). The genius in Armstrong's vocal response is evident as he instinctively chooses not to imitate Strong verbatim, but to the contrary, he vocally embellishes the melody just as an early traditional jazz clarinetist would. This immediate artistic choice is indicative of Armstrong's creative instincts born out of not only great technique but also his experiences years earlier in New Orleans. His improvised solo (see Figure 4) begins on a single note (after an anacrusis) sustained for

---

[178] This roster was the mainstay of Armstrong's Hot Seven group.
[179] See Olly Wilson's conclusions in "The Significance of the Relationship Between Afro-American Music and West African Music," referred to in Chapter I.

four measures. His aforementioned inspired creativity becomes evident when the listener realizes that despite having a plethora of melodic choices available via decades of blues music clichés, Armstrong becomes a minimalist artist and reduces his creative options to one note. Rather than playing cascading melodic lines or fanfare-type statements when he begins his improvised solo, he chose to create a contrary mood with rhythmic differentiation in an improvisational context. Hughes acknowledges and encourages such creative instincts:

> Certainly there is, for the American Negro artist who can escape the restrictions the more advanced among his own group put upon him, a great field of unused material ready for his art. Without going outside his race, and even among better classes with their "white" culture and conscious American manners, but still Negro enough to be different, there is still sufficient matter to furnish a black artist for a lifetime of work.[180]

Armstrong's keen sense of rhythm and meter is evident when what initially sounds like a variation of the initial anacrusis is repeated four times. His lyrical, rhythmic, and metric senses are distinct and varied. His improvised melodic line then becomes a statement that evolves in and out of the established meter in such a fashion that the listener gets the sense that he is reiterating the musical point made at the end of his introductory fanfare. Indeed, Armstrong mirrored Hughes's theory that "An artist must be free to choose what he does, certainly, but he must be never afraid to do what he might choose."[181] His used ornamentations to creatively use the available space as he ends his improvised, after one chorus, leaving the listener wanting more. It was as if he was affirming Hughes's admonishments two years after the fact. Hughes discussed the artist's dilemma, "But to my mind, it is the duty of the younger Negro artist, if he accepts any duties at all from outsiders, to change through the force of his art that old whispering 'I want to be

---
[180] Hughes, "The Negro Artist and the Racial Mountain," 307.
[181] Ibid., 307.

white,' hidden in the aspirations of his people, to 'Why should I want to be white? I am a Negro—and beautiful."[182] Of course, Hughes's reference here is to the antagonist in his essay. The poet's point is that just like some of the period's artists, and contrary to Armstrong's choices, the antagonist believed that the pathway to success is to create Eurocentric art. Although Armstrong had no racial pretensions in his art or disposition, his improvisation and vocalese choices in "West End Blues" affirm Hughes's admonitions as he embraced blues music's African American idiosyncrasies in Jim Crow South; the search for a collective aesthetic resulting in a responsorial existence, which requires improvisational freedom.

Armstrong's improvisational choices from the 1923 recordings with Joe "King" Oliver's Creole Jazz Band to "Blue Yodel No. 9" (with country music icon Jimmie Rodgers) in 1930 partly directed the aesthetic choices in American music. Aspiring and professional instrumental and vocal as musicians have studied and immolated his recordings with the Hot Five and Hot Seven groups in some form or fashion. A common characteristic among these artists is a propensity to make artistic choices that adhere to preset standards or follow creative urges and explore unchartered vistas. In this context, Armstrong successfully juxtaposed the dilemma, although there is no evidence that Armstrong ever met Hughes or read his essay of two years earlier. His choices in "West End Blues" mirrors the theories expressed by Langston Hughes in "The Negro Artist and the Racial Mountain." Unwittingly, Armstrong embraced (as Hughes's admonitions) the cultural uniqueness born out of blues music.

Historically, the degree of worth assigned to a single piece of art-work in any medium or a body of work from an artist or group is, in most cases, determined after the historical period has passed. It is not unusual to label art with significant posthaste. Conversely, there are measurable indicators of artistic value that appear simultaneous to the production of the art when one views the critical impact that said art has on contemporary artists. For example, Hughes, Henderson, Armstrong, Cullen, McKay,

---

[182] Ibid.

Ellington, Meta Warrick-Fuller, Hurston, and Douglas, all in varied mediums, produced works that inspired other artists to pursue their voices and contribute to the movement. These artists, in various mediums, were aware of each other's contributions contrary to the contrarian position that believed that their works of art were devoid of cross influences. Though Hughes did not mention Armstrong, Ellington, Henderson, or Waller specifically, he was conscious of the cultural impact taking place. He did, however, mention with pride the literary works of Toomer, Cullen, Roland Hayes, and Paul Robeson in his seminal essay. While not mentioning specific artists, Hughes acknowledged the importance of blues and jazz music to his literature. "But jazz to me is one of the inherent expressions of Negro life in America."[183]

Indeed, the Harlem community was also not immune to the fight for social justice as it was home to arguably two of the more divergent activist organizations, the National Association for the Advancement of Colored People, led by Du Bois, and Marcus Garvey's United Negro Improvement Association. The unique political and social climates that impacted the period's artists were too affected by the cultural environment. There were undoubtedly cross influences as blues music's rise in popularity was evident beyond Du Bois's Talented Tenth philosophy.[184] David Levering Lewis said,

> Afro-American music had always been a source of embarrassment to the Afro-American elite. The group continued to be a little annoyed by the singing of spirituals long after James Weldon Johnson and Alain Locke had proclaimed them America's most precious, beautiful, and original musical expression. Its feelings about urban spirituals—the blues—and about jazz sometimes verged on the unprintable.[185]

---

[183] Langston Hughes, "The Negro Artist and the Racial Mountain."
[184] Du Bois used the term "Talented Tenth" to describe whom he considered the best and brightest Black intellectuals.
[185] David Levering Lewis, *When Harlem Was in Vogue* (New York, Penguin Books, 1997) 173.

The music's aesthetic attraction spanned the gambit of the Black American socioeconomic spectrum. Lewis noted the significance of jazz pioneer (one of the early progenitors of the "big band ensemble" to the genre) Fletcher Henderson's role in the music's impact on the period considered here: "The Savoy jam sessions broadcast over the radio, were to American popular music what Dearborn was to transportation. Fletcher Henderson himself represented in his culture and character another significant development—the sufferance if not approval of jazz by some of the Talented Tenth."[186] Additionally, one must take note of the influence of the genre's body of work on subsequent artistic periods. Armstrong's musical approach, replete with vestiges of West African and New Orleans cultural nuances, became prevalent two decades later in the advent of bebop through the collective art of Charlie Parker, John Birks "Dizzy" Gillespie, and Thelonious Monk, the era's chief creators. One can hear recollections of Armstrong's stop-time explorations in "Texas Moaner Blues" (see Figure 1) in Parker's recording, "Parker's Mood."[187] Armstrong's rhythmic differentiation are present in many of Monk's compositions, such as "Evidence" and "Green Chimneys." Indeed, Gillespie's approach to expanding the range of the trumpet in an improvisational setting is like Armstrong's opening fanfare in "West End Blues." One can also hear the underpinnings of Armstrong's improvisational choices in Parker's composition, "Parker's Mood." More importantly, and pertinent to this discussion, Hughes acknowledged the genre's influence on his work: "Most of my own poems are racial in theme and treatment, derived from the life I know. In many of them I try to grasp and hold some meanings and rhythms of jazz."[188] Hughes was clear about what the genre meant to him: "But jazz to me is one of the inherent expressions of Negro life in America; the external tom-tom

---

[186] Ibid., 173.
[187] The chronological progression of American Jazz history includes Fletcher Henderson's "big band" creation to the small ensembles, which focused on individual soloists expanding the improvisational vocabulary. John Birk "Dizzy" Gillespie, Charlie Christian, Bud Powell, and Charlie Parker were but four of the bebop era's pioneers.
[188] Langston Hughes, *The Negro Artists and the Racial Mountain*.

beating in the Negro soul—tom-tom of revolt against the weariness if a white world, a world of subway trains, and work, work, work; the tom-tom of joy and laughter, and pain, and swallowed in a smile."[189]

The history of jazz music coincides with the history of the United States during the twentieth century. The art evolved and adapted to changing social climates and increased technological opportunities. One of the idiom's creators, "Dizzy" Gillespie, acknowledged Armstrong's importance as such, "No he, no me."[190] Miles Davis surmised that "Most of what happened up until this time in small group playing had come down from Louis Armstrong though Lester Young and Coleman Hawkins, to Dizzy and Bird, and bebop basically came from that."[191] It is also historically significant that blues and jazz music was part of the cultural debate during the Harlem Renaissance was introduced to Europe as early as 1918 by African American bandmaster and composer Lieutenant James Reese Europe and the 369th Infantry Regimental Band when they toured France during World War I. On some levels the musicians served as early period agitators. Though superb musicianship, they shared renditions of Blues Music with some of the benefactors of America's (the 369th Regiment's) role in their liberation. The "Men of Bronze" recognized America's refusal to acknowledge their bravery juxtaposed with an increase in lynching and terrorist attacks. In 1919, one year after the war's end, Sidney Bechet and Josephine Baker were a part of African American composer Will Marion Cook's Southern Syncopaters Orchestra.

---

[189] Ibid.
[190] John Birks "Dizzy" Gillespie
[191] Miles Davis, *Miles: The Autobiography* (New York, Simon and Schuster, 1989) 219.

James Reese Europe and Noble Sissle
(Schomburg Center, New York Public Library)

The group toured France, Germany, Turkey, Russia, and Istanbul. Baker received rave reviews when the orchestra became a part of a musical titled La Revue Nègre in Paris. She remained in the city when the band successfully toured most of Europe, the Near East, and Russia. Her decision to stay was salient as she unwittingly contributed to the misguided narrative that the Black American folk music was born out of savage instincts. Historian Henry Louis Gates described changes in the show's emphasis. "When the troupe reached Paris, opening night was ten days away. During that brief time the revue became more 'African,' placing less emphasis on tap-dancing and spirituals and more on Josephine Baker and her suggestive dancing."[192] Gates elaborated further:

> When the audience excitement and anticipation climaxed, Josephine Baker entered the stage in blackface lips and plaid dungarees, with knees bent, feet spread apart, buttocks thrust out, stomach sucked in, cheeks puffed out, eyes crossed. She appeared to be part animal—some people saw a kangaroo, others a giraffe—part human. Her movements were just as astonishing: shaking shimmying, writhing like a snake, contorting her torso, all this while emitting strange, high-pitched noises. Then, almost before the audience

---

[192] Henry Louis Gates, *The African-American Century: How Black Americans have shaped our Country* (New York: Simon and Schuster, 2000)

could comprehend what this apparition might possible be, she burst off-stage on all fours, stiff-legged derriere extended into the air, hands spanking the boards as she scuttled into the wings.[193]

Interestingly, while these performing artists were exposing American folk music to people recovering from the ravages of World War I, Armstrong, Ellington, and other African American musicians such as Fletcher Henderson and Thomas "Fats" Wright Waller were creating art in racially segregated venues such as the infamous Cotton Club and the Roseland in Manhattan.

In the context of the period considered here, and the decision as to whether to use one's art to "agitate or create," "Fats" Waller's 1925 composed "Black and Blue" for a Broadway musical. The song's text embraced the mental stress of spurned romantic love. In this case, the loss of a lover to a woman with less pigmentation. Armstrong chose to agitate with his rendition of the song was adopted by the Black community as a social protest, embracing the refrain "why am I so black and blue."[194]193 The transformation of "Black and Blue" from a troubled romance theme to a social statement is indicative of the consumer's consciousness.

If the epistemological critique of the period does not take into consideration the context (social and political) of the period as well as the impact on subsequent genres, the analysis is faulty at best. Charges that many of the artists adhered to their patron's aesthetic values are correct, but so did European artists Bach and Handel.[195] Yet, their body of work is considered salient to the evolution of Western performing art. Though at times on opposite ends of the continuum, Locke and Du Bois shared respect for the period's arts. They both believed that artists in any cultural era would produce works that challenge social and political norms and/or rise to an aesthetic barometer established in their community and beyond when left to their own devices. One can point to the later twentieth-century

---

[193] Ibid., 187
[194] See the lyrics to Fats Waller's *Black and Blue*.
[195] Donald Jay Grout, *A History of Western Music* (New York: Norton, 1960), 143–300.

explorations in what became known as "funk" music (often with blues music as its form) by James Brown. Indeed, the evolvement of punk rock and hip-hop in pop culture are examples of such creativity.

However, Locke's position in terms of critique and acceptance of black art was not baseless when one considers the fact that Black art is American art and subject to the whims and criticisms of those who seek to define and/or consume such creations. The question of which creative vein should African American artists choose was and still is an ever-present dilemma. Some Black artists who depended on white patrons felt pressured to produce art that would be considered acceptable. The Eurocentric barometer ingrained in American culture made it difficult for Locke not to be concerned about Black performing, literary, and visual arts' place in American and world culture. From 1925 through the end of the decade, Locke and Du Bois publicly debated the purpose and virtue of African American art. Two of the period's notable works analyzed in this chapter, "The Negro Artist and the Racial Mountain" and "West End Blues," contributed to the affirmation that the art embraces all aspects of the African American culture. Indeed, some elements of the New Negro theory put forth by Alain Locke and George Schuyler in "The Negro Art-Hokum" argue that art, which is strictly African American, is an admittance of inferiority. Consequently, artists who agreed found it challenging to produce creations that were not imitative of European precursors.

By 1925, African American blues and jazz music had become a permanent fixture in American culture with many of its creators, such as Bessie Smith and W. C. Handy residing in the Harlem community. The economic successes of their recordings, as well as their live performances, were indicative of the arts' popularity among Black and white citizens. More importantly, the values alluded to in the text of many of the songs served as a liberating aesthetic in that it recognized through music those aspects of life (failed romance, racial oppression, and job loss), which caused pain. Indeed, the first step of liberation from those life nuances is to recognize that they exist as well as their origins. Conversely, poets McKay and Hughes (whom Locke considered excellent examples of *The New Negro*) often wrote works with the blues music as its subject.[196] The popularity of the music was such that white patrons (whom Zora Neal Hurston called "negrotarians") readily attended the racially segregated venues to get as close as possible to what they perceived as African American culture. The validity of the period's critics, particularly those who were motivated by a fascination with supposed depictions of Black life, is questionable. They readily embraced the risqué presentations associated with the music while on nightly forays in Harlem. The hypocrisy lies in the fact that despite the sophistication of the performing art, its critics readily dismissed the Negro experience as happy, frolicking, and devoid of any inhibitions.[197] They were indeed outsiders who considered themselves experts on a group of artists motivated by the outsider's money. The art, politics, and philosophical debate were affected as the cultural period and all of America experienced the jolt of the 1929 Stock Market crash. Period scholar David Levering Lewis surmised that the ultimate failure of the Harlem Renaissance was inevitable: "The Depression accelerated a failure that was inevitable, for the Harlem Renaissance could no more have succeeded as a positive social force, whether the health of Wall Street, than its participants, could have been persuaded to try a different stratagem of racial advancement."[198] One should note that despite significant events such as the 1929 stock market crash and the saturation of blues music to the consuming American public, his art still flourished as a significant entity in American music. Despite the economic crash, he continued to record as a sideman and group leader.[199] The crowning point of the decade regarding his cultural influence was when, in 1930, he recorded "Blue Yodel No. 9" with country music pioneer Jimmy Rodgers. Furthermore, his 1930s recordings of Tin Pan Alley pop songs such as "Stardust," "China Town, My China Town," and "Dancing Cheek to Cheek" were similarly popular with the consuming public.

---

[196] *The Portable Harlem Renaissance Reader*, ed. David Levering Lewis (New York: Penguin Books, 1996) is an excellent source.

[197] See Rudolph Fisher's "The Caucasian Storms Harlem," *The American Mercury*, August 1927, 393–98.

[198] Ibid., 305-06.

[199] See Armstrong's discography as a leader and sideman at the end of this research.

CHAPTER V

LOUIS ARMSTRONG AND BLUES MUSIC'S IMPACT AS A FUNCTIONAL ART DURING THE HARLEM RENAISSANCE

> "I never with my eyes, saw the mistreatment of any black person. Not once…We're across the field…They sing and happy, I never heard one of them, one black person say, 'I tell you what: These doggone white people—not a word."
>
> —Phil Robertson, actor, Duck Dynasty

The early jazz music that Louis Armstrong heard as an adolescent was the result of cultural behaviors, which included performing-art practices at parades, funerals, outdoor events, and in brothels. In New Orleans, there was, and still is, the West African rooted communal approach (nonmusicians are welcome to participate), to making music with blues music as the foundation for the improvisational art form that is jazz music. Subsequently, the invention of blues music was the result of social and economic pressures put upon the African American community after the abolishment of slavery and the end of the Civil War.[200] Jazz educator and historian James H. Patterson opined: "When Africans were transported to the United States as slaves, they brought with them their culture. This meant all activities were communal and cultural for daily living, including worship/sacrifice for spiritual survival. Religion/religious customs are important to the well-being of the human spirit/soul. The blues are socio-sacred and religious in nature."[201] The implementation of Black Codes (legislative and legal measures to solidify African American persecution), terrorist reactions to Reconstruction, and the immoral practice of sharecropping became realities in a nation that had just ratified the Thirteenth, Fourteenth, and Fifteenth Amendments (guaranteeing emancipation, citizenship, and the right to vote) to the Constitution. Subsequently, work songs, just as the music of the enslaved, field hollers, and now blues music served as functional art or a conduit for coping, assistance with laborious tasks, and a mode to melancholy relief. Indeed, blues music grew (after Mamie Smith recorded "Crazy Blues" in 1920) into arguably the most popular music among Black Americans during the period considered here.

The genre, and Armstrong's instrumental and vocal contributions served as inspirations to Harlem Renaissance literary artists Langston Hughes, Zora Neal Hurston, and Sterling Brown as well as visual artists such as Aaron Douglas, Archibald Motley, and Romare Bearden. Each in their chosen mediums researched and created works with blues music and the cultural behaviors associated with it as its theme. Post-Civil War Black American migration reached all the geographic areas that had the prospects for work and/or freedom. Some of the formerly enslaved and their posterity went West and worked on the railroads. Others worked on cattle ranges in the expanding western United States and in northern factories. Still, others traveled South to seek employment on the docks of the Mississippi River in New Orleans. The work songs brought to the city by the migrating workers, along with the sacred

---

[200] See Amiri Baraka's *Blues People: Negro Music in White America* (New York: Harper Collins Publishers, 1963), 50

[201] James H. Patterson, Forward to *The Healing Properties of the Blues: Moaning, Mourning, Morning,* Sandra Foster, 2020 Library of Congress Control Number: 2019921208.

Pentecostal Protestant musical practices (that were contrary to the dominant Catholic worship services), helped create the blues music that Armstrong heard while coming of age in New Orleans. According to researcher Eileen Southern, "In keeping with their traditions, the ex-slaves sang about their experiences—their new freedom, their new occupations, the strange ways of the city, current events, and their feelings of root-lessness and loneliness."[202] Most of the work songs heard were previously performed in conjunction with the labor associated with the agrarian regions outside of the city. Many of the migrant workers in New Orleans came from the cotton fields of interior Mississippi or sugarcane fields in western and central Louisiana. Their regional music-making practices eased the intense and laborious process of planting and harvesting sugar, cotton, and tobacco, which were labor intensive and demanded worker cooperation and coordination.

The migrant workers were seeking jobs that were plentiful on the city's riverfront. They adapted the work songs used to accompany the intensive labor on plantations and sharecropper farms in their places of origin to the new urban environment, New Orleans, which was already a musical rich city. Researcher, Donald Marquis placed the importation of work songs in the context of pioneer Buddy Bolden's and performing arts' development. "The musicians who had lived on plantations and in the country brought this aspect to the city and added it to the music after Bolden had shaped the basic foundation. The field song influence was mainly a part of the later flowering of New Orleans Jazz."[203] Armstrong recalled that circa 1909, "All of a sudden came along those two great songs, 'Memphis Blues' and 'St. Louis Blues.' My they were hot and how we loved them."[204]

W. C. Handy described the music's origins as work songs with an apparatus for coordinating labor and, thus, its function as a tool for work tasks. Handy states,

---

[202] Eileen Southern, *The Music of Black Americans*, 224.
[203] Donald Marquis, *In Search of Buddy Bolden*, 37.
[204] Louis Armstrong, *Swing That Music*, 13.

> In the south long ago, whenever a new man appeared for work in any of the laborer's gangs, he would be asked if he could sing. If he could, he got the job. The singing of these working men set the rhythm for the work, the pounding of hammers, the swinging of scythes; and the one who sang most lustily soon became straw boss. One man set the tune, and sang whatever sentiments lay closest to his heart.[205]

The role of the work group's vocal leader was significant to Handy. He described the improvisational approach and the resulting call and response technique inherent in the creation of work songs: "But whatever he [the vocal leader] sang was personal, and the others in the gang took up the melody, each fitting it with personal words of his own."[206] Similarly, the worker's ancestors used the double entendre (song texts that implicitly say one thing but possess a different meaning from the producer to the receiver) technique to communicate messages covertly. Thus, the music of the field workers served to make the work tolerable while it helped to coordinate tasks requiring more than one person. In both settings, the music functioned as a performing art created beyond the purview of satisfying the desire for an absent aesthetic. Blues musician Henry Townsend described the ideological logistics of the creative process: "We all have something in mind and we didn't want to talk to anybody but the burden is real heavy until you could make some kind of sound about it, you could express yourself to somebody, sort of lighten the thing up."[207] Amiri Baraka theorized that the environmental transformation that produced the post-slavery atmosphere, reinvented the music:

---

[205] W.C. Handy, "The Heart of the Blues," *Etude Music Magazine* (March 1940): 193-94.

[206] See Olly Wilson's "The Significance of the Relationship Between Afro-American Music and West African Music," *Black Perspectives in Music* 2, no. 1 (Spring 1974): 15–22.

[207] Henry Townsend, quoted in Houston Baker Jr., *Blues, Ideology and Afro-American Literature: A Vernacular Theory* (Chicago: The University of Chicago Press, 1984), 113.

> Many Negroes who were sharecroppers, or man-aged to purchase one of the tiny farms that dotted the less fertile lands of the South, worked in their fields alone or with their families. The old shouts and hollers were still accompaniment for the arduous work of clearing land, planting, or harvesting crops. But there was a solitude to this work that had never been present in the old slave times.[208]

Beyond using music to help tolerate the laborious work-tasks at hand, Blacks were forced to carve-out an existence in a post-enslavement social order. The "solitude" element in the music that Baraka alludes to is a cultural phenomenon that embraces the performing art's power to make life in Jim Crow South tolerable, as well as the task or labor at hand easier. Baraka continued, "The small farms and share-croppers' plots produced not only what I think must have been a less self-conscious work song but a form of song or shout that did not necessarily have to be concerned with, or inspired by, *labor*."[209] The laborer/musicians discussed here imitatively used some of the same performing art techniques: call response, a communal approach, improvisation, and double entendre. Consequently, they initiated their enslaved forbearers' approach to performance (functional) art. Their art functioned as a source of relief through melancholy expressions of pain.

It is of important historical note that white composers like Hart A. Wand, a W. C. Handy contemporary, wrote many of the early blues songs. Their contributions to the genre are invaluable and crucial. However, Wand and the other White American blues music writers were not forced to live with legislated "Black Codes," and without access to constitutional guarantees and hue-inspired terrorism. Black song writers were creating a salient American music genre because of and despite of a phantom reciprocity or reward for patriotic participation in every war. The music that they and their African American counterparts

---

[208] Amiri Baraka, *Blues People: Negro Music in White America* (New York: Harper Collins, 1963), 61.

[209] Ibid., 61.

helped create is arguably one of America's salient artistic contributions to the world. For the most part, this authentic American music genre uses (mostly, not exclusively) twelve measures or increments as its foundation. However, a solo artist would often take advantage of the creative freedom and make longer segments. The result was a performing art imitative of the early vocal leaders, work gangs, and the American enslaved population. Researcher David Evans theorized that "All blues are lyrics in the sense that they are told from the first-person point of view and their emotional dimension is stressed."[210] Subsequently, their music satisfied the African American search for a collective aesthetic.

The artistry of Ma Rainey, Bessie Smith, Ethel Waters, and Louis Armstrong, among others, helped infused the desire and thus the market for blues music. It also inspired the creation of Black Swan Records. The recording company's founders converged the ideals of two Black leaders on opposite ends of a philosophical debate as to the best path for Black Americans. W. E. B. Du Bois's desire for a platform that will display the quality and depth (agitate for social change for Black Americans) is evident in his "The Criteria of Negro Art" speech. Booker T. Washington expressed a desire for Black economic empowerment years earlier when he created The Negro Business League. The company's founders were descendants of the people who helped create the music considered here. For many in the community, like Du Bois, the performing art was a striking contrast and a much-needed artistic retort to the stereotypes of minstrelsy. Notwithstanding the identification of the genre's true origins, blues music's impact was such that it satisfied an empathetic and sympathetic aesthetic quest for consumers from outside of the black community, especially those economically depressed whites. For many of them, the music satisfied a fascination and curiosity with the minstrelsy reinforced fantasies with African American culture.

Subsequently, between 1919 and 1929, millions of blues and jazz recordings were sold as recording companies explicitly created marketing divisions to take advantage of the changing aesthetics in America.

---

[210] David Evans, "Techniques of Blues Composition among Black Folksingers," *Journal of American Folklore Society* 87, no. 345 (Jul–Sep 1974): 240–49.

Moreover, before 1926, the growing blues music field was Black female-dominated, but the recording company owners, publishers, venue operators, recording studios, radio stations, artist managers, and record-store owners were predominantly male. Each had a distinct style and unique approach to the performing art.[211] Their artistry helped infuse the desire and, thus, the market for blues music.

Simultaneously, from 1923 and throughout the remainder of the period considered here, Louis Armstrong was evolving into one of America's most influential artists with seminal recordings as a vocalist and instrumentalist and the fact that he also recorded as a side-man for other blues musicians on 114 blues songs during that period is pertinent to this discussion.[212] The demand for his talents was born out of his ability to codify musical instincts that came from his experiences with the genre's New Orleans roots. Specifically, as stated before, Armstrong was product of African American folkways, and mores in arguably the nation's most unique city. The popularity of the performing art metastasized when many Blacks seeking work and relief from the oppressive South, migrated to the north during and immediately after World War I. However, the contributions of those artists who remained in the South were similarly critical, as they too impacted the performing art's growth in popularity. These phenomena are reflective of the fascination and sales of early (solo) recordings. Zora Neal Hurston's fascination led her to a role as an early proponent of the genre's penchants as she researched the performance rituals of the early primarily itinerant blues musicians who remained in the South.[213]

---

[211] Each of these vocalists had a distinctive style and became iconic figures in the early blues recordings during the period considered here.

[212] See Gilbert Erskine's essay "'Countin' The Blues: A Survey of the Recordings of Louis Armstrong Accompanying Singers in the 1920s," *Second Line,* Tulane University's Hogan Jazz Archives, New Orleans, LA.

[213] Zora Neal Hurston's *Mules and Men* (Philadelphia: J. B Lippincott, 1935), 1–4 is an exploration of cultural behaviors associated with blues music. Specifically, the music's live productions by itinerant artists and the willful participation by consumers in various settings.

It is difficult to determine specific geographical origins and the historical timeline of blues music's introduction to America's culture beyond the generic southern regions and post-Civil War years. However, most of the idiom's salient progenitors and innovators were Black. They existentially transformed the art as the music adapted in various performing settings, from solo or unaccompanied small groups and large band orchestras. Additionally, as stated earlier, the music or functional art that the Black migrant workers brought to New Orleans utilized many West African musical practices, including call response. Indeed, the work songs sung by these relocated workers were like the songs sung earlier by the enslaved. Just as the enslaved used the technique of double entendre to send secret messages, the leader or straw boss would extol or bemoan a situation at home, be it economics, trouble with a lover, or an overbearing boss. The song usually takes on the characteristic of an antiphon as the group would reply to the leader's melodic expression by imitating the stated musical line.[214] Sometimes the response remained the same, as the leader improvised new texts for every refrain.

Armstrong's contribution to music's role as a functional art is clear. He was a student/insider of New Orleans traditions and folkways. He was relatively young and just beginning his recording career during the period considered here. Biographer Thomas Brothers commented, "Armstrong's early mastery of the blues signals his position in New Orleans Society, his position in jazz history, and indeed, his position in the history of African American music."[215] His early grasp of rhythm differentiation and the performance style essential to blues music were evident in the recordings of Joe "King" Oliver's Creole Jazz Band, specifically "Chimes Blues." In addition to collaborating with early jazz artists Sidney Bechet and Clarence Williams in 1924, he joined the Fletcher Henderson Band, which was a unique musical aggregation and a precursor to what is now known as "big bands." His highly

---

[214] The Smithsonian Institute's audio recordings of prison workers and field workers by Alan Lomax are excellent examples of the antiphonal music technique in a call-response setting.

[215] Thomas Brothers, *Louis Armstrong's New Orleans* (New York: W. W. Norton, 2006), 206.

developed blues skills were evident in improvised solos. Author Bob Porter discussed the impact of the influx to New York of New Orleans musicians steeped in the blues tradition. According to Porter,

> The key performers had to leave New Orleans in order to be heard since the Crescent City had no recording industry as such. Chicago was the initial destination, but eventually Oliver, Armstrong and Morton all came to New York. Sidney Bechet, another New Orleanian, would not emerge as a leader on records until 1932, yet his fame and virtuosity were well established in New York circles in the 1920's. It was one thing to use blues in repertoire; it was another thing to be a convincing Blues [sic] soloist.[216]

Henderson and fellow bandsman/arranger Don Redman often used segments of what Armstrong played (including imitating his style) as a basis for their compositions and arrangements. Jazz historian Dan Morgenstern commented, "Redman was quick to absorb many of Armstrong's lessons. His arrangements improved considerably during Armstrong's thirteen-month stay, as did the band's rhythm and phrasing, as well as their improvisational skills."[217] Henderson and Redman's arrangement of Joe Oliver's *Dippermouth Blues*, titled *Sugarfoot Stomp*, became one of the group's more famous pieces. The listener will hear Armstrong's influence on the duo's arrangement as well as the Henderson band's enhanced musicality.

Interestingly, tenor saxophonist Coleman Hawkins, a salient contributor to the genre's history, was a member of the Henderson band and came under Armstrong's influence. Indeed, Hawkins is considered one of the early pioneers of modern jazz. His 1940 recording of *Body and*

---

[216] Louis Porter, "Blues in Jazz." ed. B. Kirchner, *The Oxford Companion to Jazz* (New York: Oxford University Press, 2000), 67–8.

[217] Dan Morgenstern, "Louis Armstrong," *Companion to Jazz*, ed. B. Kirchner, (New York: Oxford University Press, 2000), 107.

Soul helped usher in the bebop era of jazz.[218] Fellow tenor saxophonist Illinois Jacquet described the evolution as such:

> You hear a Dixieland band playing today, everybody's playing together. They're going for themselves you know. And I think what happened was that people started playing of the chord line, and started getting more progressive, then they started to realize that all those people didn't have to play together, like solos. If one was good enough then he can play without all that interruption, like Louis Armstrong. That means when you hit Coleman Hawkins, you'd hear just the saxophone and the piano and the rhythm section. Because now they were getting together, and they were playing on the chord lines.[219]

The Henderson/Redman music arrangements and compositions (filled with Armstrong's influences) subsequently reached a broader audience when bandleader Paul Whiteman (an American Caucasian conductor) introduced jazz performances and the duo's music to major, predominantly white venues across the country. Conversely, Redman, Henderson, and Whiteman heard vestiges of blues music's early proclivities. Indeed, in songs like "Sugarfoot Stomp," they codified in various mediums the style, rhythmic differentiation, and communal approach to the performing art that was present in the music from its beginnings.

The export of the functional art that is blues and jazz music to Chicago, Harlem, and the world took many routes. New Orleans jazz and blues music pioneers like Freddie Keppard, Jelly Roll Morton, and Sidney Bechet were also a part of an exodus of artists who experienced success in other regions of the country. By 1919, the New Orleans style of ragging the music, specifically the wind-instrument polyphony, was

---

[218] See Ken Burns's documentary, *Jazz: A Film by Ken Burns*, Episode Eight "Risk."

[219] Illinois Jacquet, Interview in *To Be, or Not to Bop* (Minneapolis, University of Minnesota Press, 1979) 147.

gaining notoriety across the country and abroad. Morton brought the performance art to Los Angeles, while Keppard, who also went west for a time, soon migrated north.[220] Simultaneously, Bechet began a stint with Will Marion Cook's orchestra that would take him and Josephine Baker to Europe. Interestingly, Keppard turned down an opportunity to be the first jazz band to be recorded. One of the primary conduits to the genre's popularity was the new technology. Keppard's rejection of the opportunity opened the door for the all-white Original Dixieland Jazz Band (from New Orleans) to become the first jazz band to be recorded and an early progenitor of jazz music. According to Buster Bailey, "Freddie was the original man to come out of New Orleans to New York. He had a chance to make the first jazz records—before the Original Dixieland Jazz Band—but he was afraid people would steal his tunes and arrangements, so he didn't record them.[221]

Joe "King" Oliver also departed New Orleans, taking his blues artistry to Chicago. The impact on Armstrong was profound, as he chose him (Armstrong) to take Oliver's place. Armstrong described "Kid Ory's reaction after discovering his (Armstrong's) new role: "He was a little in doubt at first, but after he looked around town he decided I was the right one to have a try at taking the great one's place. What a thrill that was! To think that I was considered up to taking Joe Oliver's place in the best band in town."[222] However, many blues musicians did not exit the South and contributed to the genre's growth and popularity. Early solo artists such as "Blind" Lemon Jefferson, Charlie Patton, and accordionist Amedee Ardoin developed their skills traveling and performing extensively in Texas, Louisiana, and Mississippi, and the genre's popularity rose infinitely among African American consumers. That popularity grew when, in 1917, the nation decided to enter World

---

[220] See Sidney Bechet's discussion in his autobiography, *Treat It Gentle* (New York: DeCapo Press, 1978), 111–14.

[221] Buster Bailey as told to Nat Shapiro and Nat Hentoff, *Hear Me Talkin' to Ya* (New York, Dover Publications, 1955) 77.

[222] Louis Armstrong, *Satchmo: My Life in New Orleans* (New York: DeCapo Press, 1954), 137.

War I and many Blacks migrated north (taking their blues music aesthetics with them) to take advantage of wartime employment.[223]

Significantly, regiment leader, Colonel William Heyward accepted the humanity of the musicians under his command who were experiencing a melancholy relief through the performing art. Colonel Hayward developed a deep admiration and respect for the black soldiers under his command and helped Europe recruit the band. According to military historian Lt. Col. Michael Lee Lanning, "Before leaving New York, Hayward had assisted Lt. James Europe in recruiting some of the finest musicians in the Northeast and secured funds from regional business leaders to buy instruments to form the regimental band. Besides increasing morale in the regiment, Europe and his musicians became known as the band that brought jazz to France."[224] Composer and Harlem Renaissance contributor Noble Sissle joined the regiment's band. After the war and Europe's untimely death, Sissle and Eubie Blake wrote many of the period's famous songs, including the short-lived and all-Black Broadway stage plays *Chocolate Dandies* and *Shuffle Along*.

Armstrong too was exporting Southern-rooted music beyond the confines of the region. In 1919, he began a stint on a Mississippi River cruise boat as the lead cornetist with the Fate Marable Orchestra. The cruise vessel's (*The Sidney*) excursions took Armstrong as far away as Davenport, Iowa, and word of his improvisational exploits traveled rapidly. Pianist Jess Stacy described hearing Armstrong on one of the excursions. "You can't imagine such energy, such musical as Louis Armstrong on that boat."[225] Armstrong's reputation as an outstanding musician was reinforced in his hometown. According to biographer Terry Teachout, "Between cruises Armstrong returned home to New

---

[223] See Amiri Baraka's discussion of this phenomenon in *Blues People: Negro Music in White America* (St. Louis, MO: Progressive Music Co., 1963), 81–94 as well as Elijah Wald's theories in *Escaping the Delta: Robert Johnson and the Invention of the Blues* (New York: Harper Collins Books, 2004), 14–42 are excellent sources. Both publications are referred to in this chapter.

[224] Lt. Col. Michael Lee Lanning, *The African-American Soldier: From Crispus Attucks to Colin Powell* (New York: Kensington Publishing Co., 2004), 139.

[225] Jess Stacy, *Riverboat Shuffle*: Cape Girardeau, Missouri 44.

Orleans, where his fellow musicians—even the Creoles of color who disdained kinky-headed players from the wrong side of town—were starting to realize that the no-longer-little Louis was a very special trumpeter indeed."[226] Many who had never heard blues music or jazz, played with the New Orleans brass band style, were astounded.

Young Armstrong had to confront one of the issues that caused the physical and cultural divide between many New Orleans musicians. The uptown area was home to predominantly improvising musicians relying on instincts, whereas their downtown, formerly trained counterparts utilized their ability to read noted music, thus expanding their venue possibilities. Armstrong said, "Later on I found out that Fate Marable had just as many jazz greats as Kid Ory, and they were better men besides they could read music and they could improvise."[227] Biographer Terry Teachout commented, "Though Armstrong knew how to read music, he had yet to work full-time with an ensemble that played written arrangements, and he saw in the offer a chance to hone his skills."[228]

The *Sydney* cruise boat and Fate Marable's band with Louis Armstrong often docked at Davenport, Iowa, the birthplace and home to one of the early critical white blues artists, trumpeter Bix Beiderbecke. The aspiring musician explored jazz and blues music as a performing art and a professional career after hearing Armstrong and the Creole Jazz Band while attending school in the Chicago area. During the Harlem Renaissance, Biederbecke was one of the first white musicians to earn notoriety for his ability to improvise blues music while in a jazz ensemble. Indeed, his development as a jazz artist and the development of other white musicians suffered as they were legally and/or culturally forbidden to play with Black musicians. Interestingly, Beiderbecke and other white musicians were hoping to learn the improvisational art from some of the genre's creators may have had their desires delayed because of the existing social order, which frowned upon integrated musical

---

[226] Terry Teachout, *Pops, A Life of Louis Armstrong*, 56.
[227] Armstrong, *Satchmo*, 182.
[228] Terry Teachout, *Pops, A Life of Louie Armstrong* (New York: Houghton Mifflin Harcourt, 2009), 48.

aggregations in the Chicago area. In 1922 and at the dawn of the period considered here, Armstrong's career received another positive lift when mentor Joe "King" Oliver recruited him to join his band in Chicago. The move to Chicago was significant as Beiderbecke, and desirous others, took advantage of Armstrong's presence and participated in after-hour music sessions, out of the watchful eyes of authorities.

Armstrong joined "King" Oliver's Creole Jazz Band as the second cornetist, and the ensemble was earning notoriety transporting the New Orleans often-outdoor, brass-band performance style to Chicago indoor venues. Unlike outdoor New Orleans jazz bands, Oliver's group did not use a sousaphone, but an upright string bass instead. For his part, Armstrong took advantage of the opportunity to match wits with his mentor. Southern blues music was at the core of the group's performance art. The young but seasoned New Orleans musicians spent most of 1922 sharing the New Orleans style of performing jazz and blues music with other curious musicians and novices. Indeed, Chicago was more than the location of Oliver and Armstrong's early successes. It was also a critical geographic spot regarding the progression of blues music's popularity in America. Many of the migrating population from the South brought blues music and the cultural behaviors associated with them to the city, while the Southern transplants were enjoying a glimpse of the culture they left behind. Armstrong was using his familiarity with Oliver's musical instincts to perfect his own improvisational and creative intuitions.[229] Armstrong said, "He willingly let me play my rendition of the Blues. Gee I was really in heaven at that particular minute. I was so happy to play for Joe and the boys."[230]

Venues such as the Lincoln Garden and the Vendome were the chief conduits for Armstrong, Oliver, and later New Orleans native brothers Johnny and Warren Dodds. Armstrong and Oliver developed a duet style of improvising that was unique and trendsetting. He also met his second wife and pianist, Lillian Armstrong, who was

---

[229] See Armstrong's comments in *Jazz: A Film by Ken Burns*, Episode Two, "The Gift."
[230] Louis Armstrong, *In His Own Words: Selected Writings* ed. Thomas Brothers (New York, Oxford University Press, 1999) 53.

instrumental in his decision to go to New York and join the Fletcher Henderson Band as well as start his groups, the Hot Five and Hot Seven. Indeed, by 1922 the Southern Black folk music or blues music was experiencing a consistent trajectory in popularity. Thus, the advent of the aforementioned "race record" divisions in the recording companies. The targeted audience identified with the indigenous music and helped the rise in the popularity of the blues.

The music progressed from mostly unrecorded solo performances to a female-dominated genre. Amiri Baraka described the transformation, "It was the first Negro music that appeared in a formal context as entertainment, though it still contained the harsh, uncompromising reality of the earlier blues forms."[231] The early recording companies, OKeh, Vocalion, Paramount, and Columbia, all took advantage of the music's rising popularity. Some of their earliest stars were Gertrude "Ma" Rainey, Bessie Smith, Trixie Smith, Ida Cox, and Sippie Wallace. The folk music also caught the attention of American mainstream white composers such as Irving Berlin, George and Ira Gershwin, and Paul Whiteman, who cashed in on the popularity of blues and jazz music. Tin Pan *Alley* music came into fruition years earlier, and the white composers' foray into the blues and jazz music genre became a part of that catalog. However, teacher, composer, musician, and musicologist W. C. Handy had misgivings about cultural outsiders becoming producers of the African American folk music. Handy explained, "I have the feeling the real blues can be written only by a Negro who keeps his roots in the life of the race."[232] Simultaneously, instrumental ensembles such as Oliver's Creole Jazz Band, Freddy Keppard's Orchestra, and the James Reese Europe Orchestra (before his untimely death in 1919) were producing blues-inspired performing art that had a potential consumer market. It did not take long for white forays into Black culture to expand beyond the performing arts.

---

[231] Ibid., 86.

[232] W. Christopher Handy, "The Heart of the Blues," *Etude Music Magazine* (March, 1940): 152, 193–94.

The Tin Pan Alley composers and artists believed they understood the mores and folkways of African Americans and could realistically contribute to the canon. Among them was *New York Times* music critic and Harlem mainstay Carl Van Vechten. In 1926, Carl Van Vechten's temerity (as well-intentioned as it may have been), inspired him to write a novel titled *Nigger Heaven*. Harlem Renaissance scholar Nathan Irwin Huggins said, "And when a white man with a reputation for sensuality, and for knowing Harlem and Negroes best, wrote a book from the 'inside,' there should have been little doubt what was looked for and what was found. The book sold 100,000 copies almost immediately. It was its pretense to be something else that made the book seem false."[233] The plot and characters were contemporaneously in Harlem. Indeed, Van Vechten became enamored with Black performing, visual and literary arts, and artists and attempted to contribute to the period's canon. He often arranged parties to facilitate a network of support by introducing artists to influential politicians, foreign visitors, and wealthy financiers. Coincidently, the author befriended African American conservative cultural critic George Schuyler, even though he (Schuyler) had a contrary view regarding the period's arts.

David Levering Lewis viewed the white patrons' fascination with Black arts as a binary phenomenon. Lewis said: "They came in an almost infinite variety. There were 'Negrotarians' who were earnest humanitarians, and those who were merely fascinated." Zora Neal Hurston coined the term "Negrotarians" to describe whites who immersed themselves in African American culture from the Harlem perspective. Lewis commented further, "By the time Nigger Heaven was released by Knopf, in August 1926, Van Vechten ('Carlo' in the inner circle) had become Harlem's most enthusiastic and ubiquitous Nordic."[234] *Nigger Heaven* and *Porgy* were two of the period's more famous works of art created by whites. More importantly, African American contributions to Black American art was ever-present during this period, and Armstrong was a consistent contributor.

---

[233] Nathan Irvin Huggins, *Harlem Renaissance*, 114.
[234] Lewis, *When Harlem Was in Vogue*, 182.

In 1923 Joe "King" Oliver and his band traveled to Indiana and recorded seven songs. It was Armstrong's first experience as a recording musician. One of the songs recorded that day was "Chimes Blues." The significance here is that Armstrong's improvised solo on "Chimes Blues" gives the listener a glimpse into the artistry that was to impact blues and jazz music. The composition utilizes what was by then a standard twelve-measure chorus with Oliver playing the melody or lead on the first five with the chimes leading the sixth one. Armstrong's solo on the seventh and eighth choruses begins a series of musical ideas fraught with the patience of a seasoned veteran, not a twenty-three-year-old transplant from New Orleans. Immediately, his rhythmic choices are executed uniquely with an element of individuality that was at the heart of blues music. Armstrong's choices are reminiscent of the music's emphasis on a solo artist's creativity. Amiri Baraka noted the music's importance: "Primitive blues had been almost a conscious expression of the Negro's *individuality* [Baraka's italics] and equally important, his *separateness*."[235] Armstrong's improvisational instincts on "Chimes Blues" mirrors Baraka's sentiments as he helped inspire a focus on the blues and jazz musician's individual contributions in an ensemble setting.

The functional art described as "classic" by Baraka was not the only performing art receiving attention in the dominant culture. Indeed, "primitive" (early) blues music practices was increasing in popularity in the South. Performing artists such as "Big" Bill Broonzey, Blind Lemon Jefferson, Petey Wheatstraw, and Charlie Patton earned attention in solo settings. Their popularity rose as they performed in traveling Black minstrel and tent shows, playing "primitive" or early blues music. Baraka described the phenomenon: "For the first time Negro music was heard on a wider scale throughout the country and began to exert a tremendous influence on the mainstream of American entertainment world..." Producers and consumers alike were enjoying unparalleled success, and the period considered here was existentially growing.

---

[235] Baraka, *Blues People: Negro Music in White America*, 86.

Much of blues music's success can be attributed to the consumer's predilection to identify with the lyrics, along with the development of an aesthetic or affinity for the performing art. Researcher Theodore W. Adorno surmised that the genre's popularity existed because of a familiarity with the standardization or constant musical form (AABA) present in most of the music consumed in America. He argued that "the whole structure of popular music is standardized, even where the attempt is made to circumvent standardization." Adorno then explained the impact on the consumer: "This inexorable device guarantees that regardless of what aberrations occur, the hit will lead back to the same familiar experience and nothing fundamentally novel will be introduced."[236] New Orleanian and gospel music icon Mahalia Jackson discussed the cultural importance the music had on her as a child: "Everybody was buying phonographs— the kind you wound up on the side by hand—just the way people have television sets today—and everybody had records of all the Negro blues singers—Bessie Smith… Ma Rainey…Mamie Smith…all the rest. You couldn't help but hear the blues."[237] The popularity of blues music was ascending to its zenith before the stock market crash of 1929, and the often-imitative recordings were helping fueling the ascent.[238]

By 1925, Bessie Smith was considered one of the most influential and popular blues artists in America. Her live concerts were consistently sold out, and they included outdoor picnics, tent revivals, lounges, and concert-hall venues. Despite her unquestionable talent as a blues artist and popularity, Pace and Handy thought her vocal style was too edgy and some of her lyrics too risqué and chose not to sign her to a recording contract with Black Swan Records. The more financially able executives at Columbia Records were willing to embrace her vocal

Bessie Smith
(Getty Images)

---

[236] Ibid., 63.
[237] Mahalia Jackson, *Movin On Up* (New York: Hawthorn Books, 1966), 29.
[238] W. C. Handy letter to Arthur Neale, February 1929, Houghton Library, Harvard University, Cambridge, MA.

style and signed her to a contract. However, the company needed help marketing their catalog of black music or "race records" and according to Armstrong biographer Terry Teachout, *Columbia Records* recruited Armstrong to accompany many of the label's blues artists including Smith:

> Shortly after Armstrong's Roseland debut, Henderson had introduced him to Frank Walker, the head of Columbia's race-record division, and Walker began using him to backup blues singers...he cut several dozen blues sides in 1924 and 1925, many of which show him off to excellent advantage—but he also played for Bessie Smith who had been recently dubbed the 'Empress of the Blues' by the *Chicago Defender*... The best known of them is a stately 'St. Louis Blues.[239]

The two giants of blues music were not personable to each other and recorded four sides together: "St. Louis Blues," "Reckless Blues," "Sobbin' Hearted Blues," and "Cold in Hand Blues." Their artistic approaches revealed an artistic schism that was hard to overcome. Armstrong was touring and receiving accolades with his Hot Five and Hot Seven groups. He was thus accustomed to the traditional New Orleans jazz approach to recorded blues productions. His musical aggregations included the traditional wind instruments' (cornet or trumpet, clarinet, and trombone) polyphony with established musical roles. Specifically, while performing blues music, each musician exchanges roles with regards to the melody, accompaniment, and soloist.[240] Indeed, he perfected his accompanying instincts during his experiences as Joe "King" Oliver's second cornetist. Smith's popularity and musical reputation were also critically acclaimed. She expressed the blues instinctively as the lead in an ensemble setting. Notably, the artist wrote many of the songs she performed and recorded. The recording reveals that Armstrong's

---

[239] Teachout, *Pops*, 90.
[240] See the discussion regarding musical roles in a traditional New Orleans Jazz ensemble in Chapter I.

artistic choices are initially responsorial and are reminiscent of not only what he heard in New Orleans, but also his recent recordings with clarinetists Sidney Bechet, Johnny Dodds, Clarence Williams's Blue Five and King Oliver's Creole Jazz Band, respectively. Smith sang four choruses, and the form was AABA. The composition uses the twelve-bar blues framework with a bridge section, followed by a return to the melody, with a predictable final cadence.

Figure 6

St. Louis Blues
(First Chorus)

W.C. Handy
Transcribed By
Michael Decuir

An analysis of Armstrong's choices reveals improvisational choices of a musician steeped in the jazz tradition of call and response. Pointedly, Smith sings the melody as is traditionally done in settings such as this, and the space created between phrases allows Armstrong the opportunity to respond. W.C. Handy described this practice of blues music productions when the lead artist (Smith) instinctively expects a response, and expectedly, Armstrong responds musically. Handy believed creative instances such as the Armstrong-Smith collaboration are examples of two specific elements in African American music:

> The first of these is a marked insistent syncopation. The second is the novel element of filling in breaks. The Negro becomes impatient with silences and fills in the rests-spaces with impromptu embellishments of his own. He slips in an 'OH Lawdy!' before the next regular beat is due. These natural improvisations are the foundations of Jazz… The grandson of the old gang worker who put in a simple 'Oh Lawdy' fills in with virtuosity on the saxophone; but both are expressing the identical racial instinct in a typically racial way.[241]

Indeed, Smith's musical offerings are short, thematic, melodic phrases separated into antecedent and consequence statements. Armstrong occupies the spaces between each statement cleverly, with disparate incomplete and complete musical ideas. He understands that he is in a trio setting, and his supportive musical role is imitative of a clarinetist's role in the New Orleans traditional brass-band setting. To this end, his responses are sensitive and contrast Smith's statements with the usual robust ornamentations characteristic of New Orleans brass band music.[242] The art of improvisation, which includes avoiding redundancy and not repeating ideas, is at the heart of jazz music and is the aquifer for this and all of Armstrong's musical endeavors.

---

[241] W. C. Handy, "The Heart of the Blues." *Etude Music Magazine*, March 1940, 152, 193–94.

[242] See measures one through eleven in Figure 6.

Subsequently, in "St. Louis Blues," Armstrong is both audacious and sensitive. In the final chorus, Armstrong recreates the approach he used during his stint with Joe "King" Oliver when he briefly abandons the responding role and harmonizes the melody with Smith. His decision to do so is bold when one considers the fact that it would have been safer to play in unison with the session's leader. The cornetist undoubtedly recalled his and Oliver's musical successes and used that recollection to avoid redundancy. Armstrong's mastery of blues music in an improvisational setting is evident when he then departs from his adventurous harmonization and returns to the traditional style of ornamentation. He uses the traditional call response to respond with the delicate sensitivity of a seasoned blues music veteran.

The functional art and its subsequent trajectory in popularity continued in the 1920s and beyond, even though many Black leaders believed it reminded them of the oppressive South and an environment they sought to escape. Still, others believed the music was not worthy of scholarly attention and thus not an accurate cultural representation for mainstream America, particularly during the post-World War I years. Activist, orator, vocalist, attorney, and stage actor Paul Robeson discussed the paradox in the context of the performance of spirituals: "Throughout the country with few exceptions, I found a contrary condition to be true. I found a special eagerness among the younger and, I am sorry to say, the more intelligent Negroes, to dismiss the spiritual as something beneath their new pride in their race."[243]244 Conversely, W.E.B. Du Bois used spiritual excerpts as chapter introductions in his 1903 publication, *The Souls of Black Folk*. Researcher Leonard Diepeveen thought that folktales did not receive acceptance: "Indeed as with spirituals, 'rediscovery may be too strong a word to apply to folktales,' for they had never disappeared as a popular oral art form. Houston Baker, Jr., surmised that the genre was difficult to comprehend because it did not earn the necessary attention from the elite: "The task of adequately describing the blues is equivalent to the labor of describing

---

[243] Paul Robeson, "Paul Robeson and Negro Music," Interview, *New York Times*, April 5, 1931, 81.

a world class athlete's awesome gymnastics. Adequate appreciation demands comprehensive attention."[244] Indeed, the Black American folk music's prominence in American culture was increasing, and African American leaders found it difficult to ignore.

To this end, blues music's place as a functional art that served as a tool for melancholy-relief, or a poignant reminder of life in the South, was making upward-mobile Blacks uncomfortable. Period literary artist and theorist James Weldon Johnson explored the aesthetic choice as a question of "high art" versus "low art." Much like Paul Robeson, he explained the inclinations of many in academia to dismiss the proclivities of folk music, particularly ragtime, one of the precursors to jazz music: "But this has been the course of scholasticism in every branch of art. Whatever new thing the people like is pooh-poohed; whatever is popular is regarded as not worth while"[245] [sic]. Levering Lewis argued, "Afro-American music had always been a source of embarrassment to the Afro-American elite. The group continued to be more than a little annoyed by the singing of spirituals long after James Weldon Johnson, and Alain Locke had proclaimed them America's most precious, beautiful, and original musical expression."[246] Beyond the music, some Black leaders chose to embrace class distinctions within their race based on pigmentation, often deepening schisms.

The differences went beyond the darker-skinned members of their community. According to E. Franklin Frazier, pride in the group's upward mobile accomplishments evolved into a superiority complex: "Not only has the distinction of blood given certain Negro groups a feeling of superiority over but it has made them feel superior to 'poor whites.' The Negro's feeling of superiority to 'poor whites' who do not bear in their veins 'aristocratic' blood has always created a barrier to any real sympathy between the two classes."[247] Samuel Floyd Jr. believed it

---

[244] Houston Baker Jr., *Blues, Ideology and Afro-American Literature: A Vernacular Theory* (Chicago: The University of Chicago Press, 1984), 4.

[245] James Weldon Johnson, *The Book of American Negro Poetry* (New York: Harcourt, Brace and Company, 1922), 13.

[246] Ibid., 173.

[247] Edward Franklin Frazier, La Bourgeoisie Noir, *Modern Quarterly* (1928): 78.

was "The demythicizing of black culture, together with the increasing separation of blacks from rural America, resulted in new tensions for African Americans who were seeking new roots and comforts."[248] However, some of the period's literary artists, notably Langston Hughes, Zora Neal Hurston, and Sterling Brown embraced, rather than ignored, reminders of life in the South. The artistic awakening forced many artists to explore the functionality of the art rather than a dismissal of Black arts in search of affirmation from the dominant Western culture. The African American communal approach to music making (which has its roots in some West African performance arts) and the aesthetic reaction to the African American performing art in a sacred setting described by Johnson, are similar to the experiences for many of the period's literary artists. Such was the case with Langston Hughes. He recognized the importance of blues music in the African American culture and, in 1925, wrote one of the period's seminal works, "Weary Blues." One year later, he published a poem dedicated to W. E. B. Du Bois titled, "The Negro Speaks of Rivers."[249] The composition earned the first-place prize from *Opportunity Magazine's* literary contest.

Succinctly, by the mid nineteen-twenties, many of Harlem's residents were transplants from the South who relocated North to escape the Jim Crow oppression and to gain employment. David Levering Lewis believed that "for the first time something of the soul of the black migrant had combined with the heart and spirit of a superior poet."[250] Indeed, Hughes's "The Weary Blues" captures the experience from the perspective of a receiver hearing a performance of blues music. Specifically, the performing art's inspiration, (which is apparent in the text of many of the blues songs) is evident to the poem's antagonist as the music (functional art) induces three essential elements, (1) empathy, (2) a consequential aftermath, (3) and a diagnosis:

---

[248] Samuel Floyd Jr., *The Power of Black Music* (New York: Oxford University Press, 1995), 89.

[249] See Lewis's discussion in *When Harlem Was in Vogue*, of Hughes's inspiration for writing *The Negro Speaks of Rivers*, 279-80.

[250] Ibid., 114.

"The Weary Blues"

Droning a drowsy syncopated tune
Rocking hard back and forth to a mellow croon,
I heard a Negro play.
Down on Lenox Avenue the other night
By the pale dull pallor of an old gas light
He did a lazy sway...
He did a lazy sway...
To the tune o' those Weary Blues...
With his ebony hands on each ivory key
He made that poor piano moan with a melody
O' Blues!
Swaying to and fro on his rickety stool
He played that sad raggy tune like a musical fool.
Sweet Blues!
Coming from a black man's soul.
O' Blues!
In a deep song voice with a melancholy tone.
I heard that Negro sing that old piano moan—
"Ain't got nobody in all this world,
Ain't got nobody but ma self.
And put my troubles on the shelf."
Thump, thump, thump, went his foot on the floor.
He played a few chords then played some more—
"I got the Weary Blues
And I can't be satisfied.
Got the Weary Blues
And can't be satisfied—
I ain't happy no mo'
I wish that I died."
And far into the night he crooned that tune.
The stars went out and so did the moon.
The singer stopped playing and went to bed
While the Weary Blues echoed through his head.
He slept like a rock or a man that's dead.

Hughes's recollection, in poetic terms, of a blues music performance, reinforces the genre as functional art. To this end, the performer uses the music to make him or her feel better. Specifically, the act affirms the cultural tradition of African Americans' use of the performing art for a melancholy relief. The formerly enslaved Frederick Douglass said, "The remark is not infrequently made, that the slaves are the most contented and happy laborers in the world. They dance and sing and make all manner of joyful noises—so they do; but it is a great mistake to suppose them happy because they sing… Slaves sing more to *make* themselves happy than to express their happiness."[251] This sentiment is reflected in lines thirty-eight and thirty-nine: "While the Weary Blues echoed through his head. He slept like a rock or a man's dead."[252] Hughes's poetic reflection of an aesthetically satisfying experience as the receiver or observer of the performing art speaks to the popularity of the music. The act of receiving or consuming art (coincidentally on Lenox Avenue in Harlem), in a familiar textual setting serves as a conduit to the satisfaction of knowing that others share the same or similar challenges (infidelity, economics, impending death) and their solutions.

Acknowledging or recognizing the sources of troubles in one's life is consistent in most of the music's themes, thus making the performing art therapeutic. Lines nineteen through twenty-two in "The Weary Blues" reflect an acknowledgment of one's troubles and a solution. "Ain't got nobody in all this world, / Ain't got nobody but ma self. / I's gwine to quit ma frownin' / And put my troubles on the shelf." Indeed, Hughes often used the same modus operandi when writing poetry with blues music as its theme. For example, Hughes's 1926 creation, "Blues Fantasy" is imitative of a blues musician's practice of expressing a vehicle for ridding oneself of a problem, then ending with the desired result. Lines twenty-four through twenty-six are an example of this compositional technique:

---

[251] Frederick Douglass, *My Bondage and My Freedom* (Boston: 1855) 96–101.
[252] See the text to *Weary Blues* referred to in this chapter.

> I got a railroad ticket,
> Pack my trunk and ride
> Sing' em sister!
> Got a railroad ticket,
> Pack my trunk and ride.
> And when I get on the train
> I'll cast my blues aside.

Albert Murray surmised:

> Applied to literature, this becomes, for me at any rate, a concern with the adequate image by which I mean the image of the hero or effective protagonist, that personification of human endeavor, if you will, which most accurately reflects the complexities and possibilities of contemporary circumstances or indeed any predicament, and also suggests its richer possibilities. In typical blues music fashion, Hughes states and re-states the situation before giving the solution or desired closure.[253]

Instinctively, the reader gets a similar sense of rhythm and flow like hearing a blues song when reading *Weary Blues* and *Blues Fantasy*. Hughes researcher W.K. Tkweme surmised,

> ...African American music, its beauty, cultural meanings, and creative representations of the people, was absolutely central to Langston Hughes's artistic project. His poetry and fiction return again and again to the figure of the black musician and scenes of music-making; his characters express themselves through traditional songs and song forms, and he pioneered in adapting the twelve-bar blues form to the printed page.[254]

---

[253] Note the practice in recordings such as *St. Louis Blues* referred to earlier in this chapter.

[254] W. S. Tkweme, "Blues in Stereo: The Texts of Langston Hughes in Jazz Music," *African American Review* 42, no.3/4 (Fall-Winter 2008): 503.

Cultural critic Thomas Dewey theorized that the consumer "must... create his own experience. And his creation must include relations comparable to those which the original producer underwent."[255] Hughes's contemporary, Sterling Brown's ode to iconic blues music pioneer, Ma Rainey, confirms Dewey's theory.[256] The third stanza codifies the perspective of the art's receiver:

> O Ma Rainey,
> Sing yo song;
> Now yous back
> Whah you belong,
> Git way inside us,
> Keep us strong...
> O Ma Rainey,
> Lil' an low;
> Sing us 'bout de hard luck
> Roun' our do';
> Sing us bout de lonesome road
> We mus' go...

Houston Baker Jr. described Brown's decision to abandon a Eurocentric model for the poetic verse as such:

> A college bred man like Sterling Brown, standing as a member of a second (or even third) twentieth century Afro-American intellectual generation, could readily set himself of knowing the score where the folk national (blues) voice was concerned. The inroads on myths and shibboleths, nonsense and exclusion, made by a first (and perhaps second) generation ensured Brown the necessary emotional and intellectual confidence

---

[255] Thomas Dewey, *Art as Experience* 60.
[256] *The Collected Poems of Sterling Brown*, ed. Michael Harper (Evanston: Northwestern University Press, 1980), 62.

to mine a southern Afro-American tradition with dedicated genius.[257]

Biographer JoAnne V. Gabbin discussed Brown's homage to the blues music great as such:

"Brown skillfully brings together the ballad and blues forms and, demonstrating his inventive genius, creates the blues-ballad."

Interestingly, many blues musicians chose not to migrate north to otherwise attractive urban areas. They served as a source for writers and researchers exploring the cultural impact, the nuances of the genre, and in the context of early performing practices.[258] To this end, early blues music progenitors, Charlie Patton, Lemon Henry "Blind" Lemon Jefferson, and T-Bone Walker were three that became prominent artists during the first three decades of the twentieth century.[259] Other seminal artists included "Big" Bill Broonzy, "Leadbelly" Ledbetter, and Robert Johnson, were prominent during the years Zora Neal Hurston researched and documented the music, mores, and folkways associated with southern African American culture. Hurston's 1935 research discussed in a previous chapter titled *Mules and Men* was a sociological study of the music and the folkways associated with the culture. Similarly, anthropologist and musicologist Alan Lomax focused much of his ethnomusicological research on southern African American folk music by often recording the folk music in its inherent rural setting.

Though many of the genre's notable artists chose to remain in the South and perform their art as itinerant musicians, the behaviors and aesthetic satisfaction associated with the function of the music were

---

[257] Houston Baker Jr., *Modernism and the Harlem Renaissance* (Chicago: The University of Chicago Press, 1987), 92.

[258] Joanne V. Gabbin, *Sterling Brown: Building the Black Aesthetic Tradition* (Charlottesville: The University of Virginia Press, 1985), 157.

[259] The artists noted here and in the next sentence were but a few who signed recording contracts and assigned to the "race record" division.

not lost on the recently migrated urban African Americans. According to Amiri Baraka, "The South was *home*. It was the place Negroes knew, and given the natural attachment of man to land, even loved."[260] Theoretically, the fictional musician Hughes describes in *The Weary Blues* is perhaps an itinerant artist who may be in a rural venue or at one of Harlem's notorious rent parties or perhaps in a cabaret setting. The point is, the artist satisfies a black aesthetic through a reciprocal association with the song's texts, resulting in a melancholy relief.[261]

From the recording industry's perspective, the folk music whose roots are in the spirituals, work songs, and sacred worship songs was rapidly becoming the most popular genre in America, and there was an opportunity to market these ethnic-specific recordings to a diverse group of consumers. Consequently, "race-record" recordings tried to capture the performer's or insider's perspective particularly when the art adopts the problem-solution format (to the satisfaction of the consumers) creating blues music as a functional art. Subsequently, the opportunity presented itself in hundreds of blues music songs. Southern itinerant blues artist, Lemon Henry "Blind Lemon" Jefferson's 1925 composition, "See That My Grave Is Kept Clean" is an excellent example of problem-recognition-solution compositional technique:[262]

> Just one kind favor I ask of you
> One kind favor I ask of you
> One kind favor, I ask of you
> See that my grave is kept clean
> See that my grave is kept clean

---

[260] Ibid., 105.

[261] Hosting a party at one's apartment and charging an entrance fee was a popular way to raise the money necessary to pay the rent. Documentation of such parties is widely published in works such as David Levering Lewis's *When Harlem Was in Vogue*, 198–239 and George Schuyler's "The Negro Art-Hokum," 96.

[262] Lemon Henry "Blind Lemon" Jefferson, recorded October 1927 for "See That My Grave Is Kept Clean" in 1927 for Paramount Recording Company. 78 rpm.

In "See That My Grave Is Kept Clean," Jefferson is contemplating the inevitability of his death and concerned his post-life legacy. Specifically, whether he has lived a life worthy of significant remembrance. To this end, Jefferson makes a specific request that his friends periodically clean his grave, ensuring his place in their memory. Subsequently, the song functions as therapeutic when it is used in a performance setting and gives the producer and the receiver an expected melancholy relief. Similarly, when the music of the enslaved was presented in post-slavery settings during this became a functional art during this period. Cultural theorist Samuel Floyd Jr. discussed the reciprocity apparent when some hear Black music: "With the musical experience, the expectation is that something musical will happen in the playing of music, and it is the *something* that fascinates, that elevates the expectation and places the hearer in a critical mode." Hence, the performing art as therapy is nothing new.[263]

"Blind" Lemon Jefferson
(Public Domain)

The inspiration associated with blues music-making is imitative of the performing art created from the enslaved Africans who were coming to grips with the reality of the loss of freedom, when they expressed their unhappiness in music and received a melancholy relief. The use of music as a functional art continued when the enslaved cleverly used melodic

---

[263] See John Blacking Jr.'s *How Musical Is Man?* (Seattle: The University of Washington Press, 1973), 3–31.

texts to covertly inform each other of planned escapes while keeping a suspicious overseer at bay. They used code words like "ain't gonna study war no more" or "O Canaan, sweet Canaan… I ain't got long to stay here."[264] To those who are outside of the experience, it may have meant a speedy summons to heaven. To others, it meant contemplation of an escape to the north. The texts of these songs served as a double entendre similar to some risqué lyrics of early blues music.[265]

Succinctly, the music/functional art inspired Langston Hughes, Zora Neal Hurston, and Sterling Brown and period literary artists to capture through texts the receiver's relationship with the performing art. When placed in the context of Dewey's theory, blues music consumers bring a degree of familiarity and expectations when experiencing performances either live or via race records. The result was a trajectory in popularity that was reflected in record sales. To this end, Louis Armstrong became one of the genre's most prolific artists. His contributions were significant both as a vocalist and instrumentalist. Armstrong has an extensive body of work as an accompanist on 114 recordings for dozens of blues artists.

Zora Neal Hurston Sterling Brown
Schomburg Schomburg
(Center, New York Public Library)

---

[264] Many narratives of the enslaved such as Frederick Douglass's *My Bondage and My Freedom* discuss the use of texts to communicate plans of escape secretly. The practice known as double entendre continued in the creation of blues music.

[265] "My Handy Man," sung by Alberta Hunter, is an excellent example of the use of double entendre. The text of the song discusses the way the handyman can satisfy the areas that need attention though the words are about a man who works around the house, they could be interpreted as a request and obliging of sexual favors.

Additionally, Armstrong's artistry was on display in dozens of recordings as a leader and a sideman. His professional career is juxtaposed with the fact that blues music assumed the role of functional art, serving the needs of relief and/or problem-solving while entertaining its consumers. The performing art's uniqueness is recognizable when one analyzes the enslaved African's use of musically transmitted coded messages. The music functions therapeutically when a solo artist gains a melancholy relief from the purview of his or her surroundings, which was usually absent from an audience. When performed in the presence of a consuming public, the music elicits empathy and generates feelings of hope that come with identifying solutions. Indeed, the genre originated from a purely functional art such as work songs created to make tasks more manageable. The consumer and producer created coping mechanisms and solutions to their collective or personal social ills.

CHAPTER VI

LOUIS ARMSTRONG, THE NEW NEGRO PHILOSOPHY, AND BLUES MUSIC IN AMERICAN CULTURE

"If he invited me to a public hanging, I'd be on the front row."
Then candidate, now U.S. Senator, Mississippi, Cyndy Hyde-Smith

Often, the designating or labeling of artistic periods happens in a historical context, such as the beginnings of the cultural movement discussed here. The *New Negro* sentiment has its roots in the essays and protests that appeared decades before the Harlem Renaissance.[266] Pertinent to the discussion here, it is telling that by the beginning of World War I, African American leaders found themselves debating the extent of Black American participation in the American war effort.[267] William Monroe Trotter opposed such an

---

[266] Ida Barnett Wells's campaign against lynching and terrorism is an excellent example of resistance to the status quo. Her publication, *The Truth About Lynching*, is an excellent example of her desire to expose to the world the incidents and accusations of interracial sex as the prime factor inspiring violence against blacks.

[267] Some leaders thought that volunteering for the war would confirm a sense of patriotism, guaranteeing many sought-after civil freedoms. Others felt that

undertaking, but Du Bois, who by now embraced the socialist ideology, saw the opportunity to fundamentally change (through patriotic Black American military participation) the postwar Eurocentric hold on art, music, history, and philosophy. After the sinking of the ship *Lusitania* (one of the catalysts for American involvement in the war), Du Bois opined,

> Well civilization has met its Waterloo. The civilization by which America insists on measuring us and to which we must conform our natural tastes and inclinations is the daughter of that European civilization which is now rushing furiously to its doom. 'What good came come out of it all?' Old standards of beauty beckon us again, not the blue-eyed, white-skinned types which are set before us in school and in literature but rich, Brown and black men and women with glowing dark eyes and crinkling hair. The sooner the rotten edifice of racism and class exploitation rumbled the world would be bathed in a golden hue that harks back to the heritage of Africa and the tropics.[268]

Interestingly, the exhibition of bravery by African American soldiers in all the previous wars, even when faced with restraints from their constitutional rights, was not enough to exercise any leverage against Du Bois's initial pacifist position with the Socialist Party. However, he understood the benefits of creating a Black officer's training program at the behest of fellow NAACP official, Joel Spingarn. Writer Archibald Grimke and activist William Monroe Trotter were skeptical of the postwar promises made to Black Americans and fellow Socialists Asa Randolph and Chandler Owen were skeptical of Du Bois's increasing enthusiasm for the war.

---

because of the mistreatment of black veterans in places like Houston, African Americans should not participate in the war effort.

[268] W. E. B. Du Bois

The success of the Des Moines Black Officer Training Camp withstood the consistent onslaught of racist propaganda initially designed to maintain the institution of slavery and later to justify Jim Crow laws. Black leaders found themselves arguing for inclusion in the military with government officials continuously guided by an American culture that saw African Americans as lazy, cowardly, and intellectually lacking any leadership capabilities. Lt. Col (Ret) Michael Lee Manning described the dilemma as such:

> Despite their outstanding service in Mexico and their long record of brave performance in previous wars, the four black regiments did not receive orders to Europe after the declaration of war because many senior military and political leaders still believed that African Americans lacked the intelligence, courage, and dedication to serve in sustained combat roles. These same leaders maintained that both the army and navy should limit blacks to menial positions as laborers and servants, and many continued to question whether blacks should serve at all.[269]

Consequently, a cultural paradox existed when the folk music of Black Americans began an upward trajectory in American popular music while African Americans were again displaying bravery in military conflicts abroad with a renewed aggregate demand for freedom at home under the guise of the *New Negro*.[270] Levering Lewis described the African American optimism after successful efforts to create an officer training school for black soldiers: "This time the lynching must cease, the ballot booth open, and jobs go to anyone who could work.

---

[269] Lt Col (Ret) Michael Lee Manning, *The African-American Soldier: From Crispus Attucks to Colin Powell* (New York, Citadel Press, 2004), 120-21.

[270] W. E. B. Du Bois, among others, expressed the frustrations of many returning black veterans with the inability to enjoy the same freedom they fought to ensure in Europe. His poem "Returning Soldiers" is an example of the "New Negro" decision to respond in kind to acts of terrorism.

And this time, Black men must be led into battle by Black officers."[271] The impending American involvement in the war made it evident that the fight for freedom in America was intrinsically tied to the struggle for freedom the world over, and to Du Bois, an opportunity to remove the colonial hegemony.

In "The Criteria of Negro Art" speech and the *New Negro* publication, Du Bois and Locke respectively expressed both pride and concern regarding the direction of African American arts. Du Bois desired a body of work (visual, literary, and performing arts) that is indicative of Black life in America. Locke argued that acquiescing to Euro standards is necessary for acceptance into the broader consumer market. Beyond coincidence, Louis Armstrong simultaneously became one of America's significant progenitors (through over one hundred recordings as a sideman and thousands of live performances) of its artistic contributions to the world of blues and jazz music. Though one could argue that the two realities could be divergent, the fact remains that Armstrong, Du Bois, Locke, and every other citizen of color lived in a nation that defended democracy in Europe (to which Blacks fought with distinction) but refused to pass an antilynching bill or guarantee constitutional rights to its Black American citizens.

Fantasies of civil rewards after participating in the war were born out of an incessant idea that continued acts of bravery in military battle would finally guarantee freedom. Despite the relatively recent heroics of African American soldiers during the Spanish-American War, some in the War Department, to whom Manning referred to, still believed it was foolhardy to include African Americans in the war effort. In contrast, some Black war veterans chose to express a *New Negro* sentiment through community activism. Louis Armstrong's mentor, Spanish-American War veteran, and headmaster of the Colored Waifs Home for Boys, founder Joseph Jones was "fresh from duty in the tenth, and he drilled the boys every morning with wooden guns"[272] Jones's patriotic fervor never swanned, and he expected the same level of duty

---

[271] David Levering Lewis, *When Harlem Was in Vogue* 8.
[272] Thomas Brothers, *Louis Armstrong's New Orleans*, 101.

and honor from his students. The desire to prove Black American worth through patriotism inspired decisions to join the war effort. Dr. Joseph Holley mirrored Captain Jones's patriotic (New Negro) sentiments. He and the entire male faculty at the Albany Bible and Manual Training Institute, volunteered to serve in the US Army during WWI. All but Dr. Holley (age restraints) fought with the 369th Regiment.

Tracing the origins of the *New Negro* sentiment is difficult. Relative to the period researched here, many were aware of the heroic exploits of Sergeant Henry Johnson during his tour of duty the 369th Regiment during World War I. Johnson single-handedly killed four of the enemy and captured twenty-two, after suffering several bullet wounds and running out of ammunition. However, countless acts of bravery on the battlefield and civil disobedience has its origins before the arrival of the first enslaved in 1619. Indeed, every act of defiance and resistance, like the slave uprisings in Louisiana that were discussed in Chapter I, or Robert Small's, heroic exploits in South Carolina at the dawn of the Civil War and Josephine Decuir's defiance of segregated seating laws on a New Orleans steamboat are vestiges of a *New Negro* attitude. Similarly, New Orleans native Homer Plessey's legal fight to desegregate the city's public transit apparatus is representative of the New Negro sentiment. Significantly, the court's decision in the landmark Plessey v. Ferguson case affirmed separation based upon race and was far-reaching as it impacted race relations in America well into the twentieth century. However, to identify the immediate impact on the Harlem Renaissance this writer will explore more recent (relative to the first decades of the twentieth century) events and more importantly, the efforts which included terrorist acts to suppress such quests for freedom, even after fighting to guarantee the same freedoms on other continents.

Curiously, one can find the *New Negro* attitude in the all-Black Ninth and Tenth Cavalries' heroics under the command of Lieutenant Colonel Charles Young. Optimism in the ranks of Black leaders was obvious as they believed military participation would and should move the quest for equality forward. Less than a decade before America's entry into WWI, Lieutenant Colonel Charles Young and Black soldiers under his command played a major part in the defeat of Pancho Villa.

Specifically, Villa was an enemy to the governments of Mexico and the United States, and the insurrectionist was the subject of an intense pursuit, and Young's bravery played a large part in Villa's demise. Villa sought to overthrow the Mexican government by involving American military forces in a border war. The year was 1916, and the Ninth and Tenth Cavalries surrounded approximately one hundred fifty of Villa's revolutionaries, and under cover of machine-gun fire, the all-Black Buffalo Soldiers killed and scattered their combatants. It was the first time the American military used the new weapon in war.[273] The defiant courage of the soldiers who refused to accept lower-class status after risking their lives fighting a war to guarantee freedoms for other groups is also indicative of the *New Negro* attitude.

The bravery of the Buffalo Soldiers was not lost on period literary artist James Weldon Johnson when he wrote "The Color Sergeant." David Levering Lewis described the poem as "a comment on the historic patriotism of African Americans and the historic ingratitude shown them by white Americans."[274] Indeed, spirits were high, and optimism abounded at the end of the World War I, and the nation seemed poised to honor the Black war heroes in much the same spirit it traditionally does for Caucasian military honorees. However, the soldiers and most of Black America experienced what Langston Hughes described as a "dream deferred."

---

[273] The heroics of African American soldiers are chronicled in Lieutenant Colonel (retired) Michael Lee Lanning's publication, *The African-American Soldier: From Crispus Attucks to Colin Powell* (New York: Kensington Publishing Company, 2004), 129–48.

[274] David Levering Lewis, Introduction to "James Weldon Johnson," *The Portable Harlem Renaissance Reader,* ed. David Levering Lewis (New York: PenguinBooks, 1999), 279.

James Weldon Johnson
(Schomburg Center, New York Public Library)

One may identify the *New Negro* guise in Du Bois's views regarding the struggle for civil rights in America. The leader believed that the fight was a part of a global struggle against colonialism, particularly in Africa. In 1916 at the onslaught of the war, he published an essay in the *Crisis* magazine titled "The African Roots of the War." The essay was an expose' revealing how the European military powers and war combatants France, Germany, and Italy had successfully used citizens of Algeria, Abyssinia, Somalia, South Africa, and West Africa. Nations who paradoxically were victims of the colonization and new political boundaries established to defend their military on the conquests on the continent at the Berlin Conference of 1883.[275] According to Lewis:

> Du Bois passed in kaleidoscope review the ravages of African history from the earliest times to the European Renaissance, Stanley's two-year charge from the source of the Congo River to its mouth in 1879, the partition five years later of the continent at the Berlin Conference, and the miasma of Christianity and commerce suffocating indigenous cultures and kingdoms. European hegemony based on technological superiority had produced the "color line," which became the thought synonymous with inferiority.[276]

---

[275] Ibid.
[276] David Levering Lewis, *W. E. B. Du Bois: Biography of A Race*, 504.

Subsequently, African American as well as African participation in the war was valiant. Harlem's 369th Regiment, called the "Men of Bronze," proved that bravery and patriotism were just as prevalent in their ranks as any other. Significantly and pertinent to the discussion here, the regiment's band led by Lieutenant James Reese Europe introduced blues music to many European citizens who heretofore had never heard the American performing arts genre.

In 1918 Du Bois organized the second Pan-African Conference in London partly because of the steady decline in race relations (including increasing terrorist attacks), the treatment of returning Black soldiers, and an increasing disregard for the problems of people of color throughout the world. He recognized that the shortcomings in the American and European educational system regarding non-Western history, particularly Africa's contribution to world history, were contributing factors to the continued post-war European colonization. Du Bois, Arnold Schomberg ("The Negro Digs Up His Past"), Carter G. Woodson ("The Mis-Education of the Negro") and others all recognized the inherent problem with an education system that does not acknowledge the contributions to history from a significant segment of the population it is supposedly serving. Du Bois contributed to the canon with a series of essays and analyses assailing America's race problem. *The Souls of Black Folk* (written in 1903) and later "The Souls of White Folk" outlined the economic disadvantage of low wages or cheap labor present in Western nations and colonized areas around the world. More profound, and pertinent to Woodson's and Schomberg's admonitions, was his argument that historical Africa was the foundation for the greatness of Europe. According to biographer David Levering Lewis, Du Bois was unrelenting: "Conceding the superiority of European cultural achievements to 'any culture that arose in Asia or Africa,' Du Bois discounted Europeans as the reason for these achievements."[277] Du Bois's attitude toward colonialism and wage disparity fueled his embracement of socialism, and were views he repeatedly expressed throughout the remaining decades of his life.

---

[277] David Levering Lewis, *W. E. B. Du Bois: The Fight for Equality and the American Century, 1919-1963* (New York: Henry Holt and Company, LLC, 2000), 15.

Carter G. Woodson
(Schomburg Center, New York Public Library)

The post-war optimism that was fueling the neo-*New Negro* sentiment was somewhat generated by the success of the blues music played by the Black regiment's band led by James Reese Europe. Pertinent to the *New Negro* philosophy, Europe successfully infused ragtime and blues music into American popular music.[278] Europe group played his compositions and arrangements of traditional songs like W. C. Handy's "St. Louis Blues." Moreover, one of the most telling and poignant songs recorded by Reese's Hell Fighters' band was "How Ya Gonna Keep 'Em Down on the Farm (After They've Seen Paree)?" The lyrics suggest that Black soldiers are justified in demanding freedom at home after granting liberty in Europe. Levering Lewis discusses the band's triumph as a part of the Hell Fighters:

> Big Jim Europe's band, its instruments bought through a tin can millionaire's generosity, conquered French, Belgium and British audiences as utterly as his regiment overwhelmed Germans in battle, leaving crowds delighted and critics mystified by the wah-wah of the "talking trumpet." (So much so that when the proud skilled musicians of France's Garde Republicaine failed to re-produce these unique sounds, suspicious experts examined one of Europe's horns for some hidden valve or chamber).[279]

---

[278] See video documentarian Ken Burn's Jazz: *Episode Two: The Gift.*
[279] Lewis, *When Harlem Was in Vogue*, 3.

Simultaneously, Louis Armstrong and other migrating New Orleans jazz musicians (Joe Oliver, Freddie Keppard, Sidney Bechet, and "Jelly Roll" Morton among others) were harnessing improvisational techniques (heretofore underused in Western art forms) that were foreign to the European and American orchestral medium.

Optimism, pride, and patriotism abounded when activist Asa Phillip Randolph wrote an essay titled "A New Crowd—A New Negro." Randolph cautioned, "Before it is possible for the Negro to prosecute successfully a formidable offensive for justice and fair play, he must tear down his false leaders, just as the people of Europe are tearing down their false leaders."[280]

The city of New York decided to honor Europe and returning Black American war veterans, and on February 17, 1919, the city staged a ticker-tape parade from Manhattan north to Harlem. Lewis describes the city's show of appreciation for the "only unit of war allowed to fly a state flag, the only American unit awarded the Croix de Guerre, and, as the French High Command's supreme mark of honor, the regiment chosen among the allied forces to lead the march to the Rhine."[281] Lewis further notes the heroic excitement that the parade generated. "Colonel Hayward and Lieutenant Europe (the sole African American officer) were objects of special attention by the crowds, but the hero of the moment was a coal dealer from Albany, Sergeant Henry Johnson, the first American to win Croix de Guerre (star with palm) gleamed from the sergeant's tunic as he stood waving graciously, in the open limousine provided by the city."[282] Europe extolled the virtues of America's new music, its uniqueness, and the way it helped develop racial pride. In 1919 months before his death, Lieutenant Europe discussed the African American and nationalistic musical approach and the creative instincts involved: "The negro loves anything that is peculiar in music and this 'jazzing' appeals to him strongly."[283] He further explained the

---

[280] Asa Phillip Randolph, *A New Crowd-A New Negro* New York: The Messenger, Vol II May–June 1919.

[281] David Levering Lewis, *When Harlem Was in Vogue*, 4.

[282] Ibid., 3–24.

[283] James Reese Europe, "A Negro Explains Jazz," *Literary Digest* (April 26, 1919): 28–9.

band's popularity in France and their unique musical approach to the performing art:

> We won France by playing music which was ours and not a pale imitation of others, and if we are to develop in America we must develop along our own lines. Our musicians do their best work when using negro material. Will Marion Cook, William Tyers, even Harry Burleigh, and Coleridge Taylor, are only truly themselves in the music which expresses their race. Mr. Tires for instance writes charming waltzes, but the best of these have in them Negro influences. The music of our race springs from the soul and this true with no other race, except possibly the Russians and it is because of this.[284]

One could argue that Europe's musical exploits were artistic expressions of the *New Negro* sentiment. He successfully codified and presented relatively new American music genres in contrast to the minstrel stereotypes.

369th on Parade (National Archives)

---

[284] Ibid., 28–9.

The musicians Europe listed in his discussion all went on to become contributors to the performing arts during the period considered here. Cook and Tyers were his assistants and performed a triumphant postwar concert tour in several European cities. Before the war effort, Burleigh was a noted collector and progenitor of African American spirituals and shared them with his music conservatory teacher Antonin Dvorak who in 1892 wrote "From the New World Symphony." The piece was America's attempt at a nationalistic composition. Coleridge-Taylor was to become one of the twentieth century's outstanding composers.[285] However, despite the contributions of some of the period's early seminal artists, and more importantly, the courageous exploits of the "Men of Bronze," they and most of Black America experienced heightened bigotry and terroristic acts by those who would otherwise wish to maintain the post-Reconstruction and pre-World War I social order. Black participation in the war effort was of no significance to them. Save the New York City parade, Black American contribution to the World War I effort was marginalized by the United States government and not included in academic history books. Save the adamant Black leaders who were dedicated African American inclusion in the constitutional guarantees, the *New Negro* sentiments were lost on the nation's and state's governing bodies.

Indeed, the postwar optimism that was a part of the *New Negro* sentiment was high when Du Bois spearheaded the first Pan-African Congress in Paris. President Woodrow Wilson's fourteen-point peace plan included a global "right to self-determination."[286] Du Bois and other delegates, particularly those from Africa, saw the proclamation as the beginning of the end of decades-long colonialism and the implementation of civil rights in America. However, the congratulatory and celebratory atmosphere for the Men of Bronze at war's end was short-lived. The leading terrorist organization in America, the Ku Klux Klan, increased its murderous acts of lynching Black Americans, and

---

[285] See Eileen Southern's discussion of the musicians in *The Music of Black Americans* (New York: W. W. Norton & Co., 1997), 357–58.

[286] Woodrow Wilson published his fourteen-point plan for peace in 1918. Specifically, number V addresses the desire for the postwar peoples' right to self-determination.

the summer of 1919 witnessed some of the worst race riots in the nation's history. David Levering Lewis described the hostile atmosphere: "The year 1919 was less than seven weeks old when the 369th Infantry Regiment marched proudly up Fifth Avenue. By the end of 1919, there had been race riots in two dozen cities, towns, or counties, rampant lynchings [sic], and resurrection of the Ku Klux Klan, and a dismal falling off of jobs in the North for Afro-Americans."[287] Consequently, fantasies of African American (and women) full citizenship in America dissipated when Black soldiers returned to a renewed Jim Crow setting. The ruling class was unmoved by any acts of patriotism that was on display by the descendants of African slaves. Du Bois eloquently expressed the collective Black American frustration:

> The faults of our country are our faults. Under similar circumstances, we would fight again. But by the God of heaven, we are cowards and jack-asses if now that the war is over we do not marshal every ounce of our brain and brawn to fight a sterner, longer, more unbending battle against the forces of hell in our own land. We return. We return from fighting. We return fighting. Make way for democracy! We saved it in France, and by the great Jehovah, we will save it in the United States of America, or know the reason why.[288]

The frustration manifested into aggressive actions as Blacks across America began retaliating against terrorist attacks. Consequently, the growing sentiment and human instinct (which was always there) of fighting back and defending their communities increased. Lewis commented,

> The Red Summer and its aftermath forged a different leadership, however. Washington D.C. and Chicago had shown how little fear of white men there was among

---
[287] Lewis, *When Harlem Was in Vogue*, 23.
[288] W. E. B. Du Bois, "Returning Soldiers," *Crisis Magazine* (1919): 14.

demobilized Afro-American soldiers or peasants who had braved the unknown of migration. Now from the lips of virtually every spokesman and the pages of every publication there was suddenly not only a bold new rhetoric—there was a "New Negro."[289]

Violence inspired by racial tensions did not escape historian Carter G. Woodson who narrowly escaped death when he happened upon the beating of some Blacks at the hands of a mob in Washington, DC. If not for the courage of two white women who recognized the gravity of the situation and hid Woodson with their bodies in the doorway of a storefront, he too may have been killed or injured by the mob.[290]

Months after the parade honoring the "Men of Bronze," the nation experienced some of the heretofore worse racial violence. The events were relative precursors to the *New Negro* sentiment. In Longview, Texas, Black cotton farmers, inspired by the prospects of economic liberty as expressed by Booker T. Washington's National Negro Business League, decided to negotiate their market prices. When the widely circulated black newspaper the *Defender* based in Chicago, publicized the details of a Longview lynching of a young Black man, the city's ruling class blamed two of the organization's leaders, S. L. Jones, and C. P. Davis, for submitting the details to the periodical. Racial tensions exploded when a mob of white terrorists physically attacked the leaders and demanded that they leave town. The Black farmers decided to resist and defend themselves and their families and heeded a call to arms. The armed group assembled at Davis's home, anticipating an attack by the White mob. The mob attacked the leader's home and when the defenders returned fire, four of the terrorists were dead. The governor declared martial law and sent the militia in after whites went on a violent rampage and burning spree. Weeks after the Longview riots, several Black youths were swimming and paddling in Chicago's Lake Michigan. The youths were taking advantage of an accessible leisure

---

[289] Lewis, *When Harlem Was in Vogue*, 24.
[290] Ibid., 19.

behavior enjoyed by the city's white residents, all seeking relief from the summer's heat. The Black bathers crossed an imaginary racial boundary and swam where white swimmers were. Eugene Williams was mortally injured when he suffered a head injury from one of the rocks thrown by an angry mob. The seventeen-year-old drowned. There were no arrests, and like the Longview incident, the absence of justice under the law inspired reactions and counterreactions. Racially motivated mobs killed fifteen whites and twenty-three Blacks, injured six hundred, and more than a thousand Black residents' homes were torched. Juxtaposed with the obvious and overt acts of terrorism against them were the seemingly perpetual judicial setbacks. More important is the adaptation of the 'problem-acknowledgment-solution' paradigm. One of the salient outgrowths of the landmark Plessey v.

Ferguson Supreme Court decision sanctioning racial segregation was the creation of economically viable and self-sufficient Black communities. Subsequently, racial pride surged after the summer of 1919, and it manifested itself in urban areas that were experiencing an upsurge in Black citizens who were relocating from the South to cities like Chicago, Detroit, and New York, particularly the northern Manhattan neighborhood, Harlem. Du Bois called Harlem home, as did the headquarters of the National Association for the Advancement of Colored People, which evolved from the Niagara Movement. Harlem was also the home of the Urban League, and some of the largest African American churches in the nation. According to author Amy Helene Kirschke, "Harlem was a city within a city, one of the most beautiful and healthy sections of the city, with its own churches, social and civic centers, shops, theaters and other places of amusements. It contained more Negroes per square miles than any other place on earth, beginning on 125th Street and covering twenty five solid blocks."[291] NAACP executive secretary James Weldon Johnson described Harlem as a "Negro metropolis, the mecca for the sightseer, the pleasure seeker, the curious, the adventurous, the enterprising, the ambitious, and

---

[291] Amy Kirschke, *Aaron Douglas: Art, Race, and the Harlem Renaissance* (Jackson: The University of Mississippi Press, 1995), 23.

the talented of the Negro world."²⁹² African American war veterans recognized the hypocrisy of fighting for democracy in Europe and returning to a nation that not only condoned Jim Crow laws and racial apartheid but also refused to acknowledge and address the terrorist act of lynching. After proving their bravery and patriotism in yet another war, they and their communities continued to suffer denial of the rights guaranteed by the United States Constitution and pursuit of happiness. Ironically, and in the context of the New Negro sentiment, the peace agreement ending the war was signed in the country that acknowledged their heroics, France. The treaty inspired a period of neo-nationalism in Eastern Europe, which led to new geographical/political boundaries creating such new nations such as Yugoslavia and Hungary. Indeed, a few years later, returning German World War I veteran Adolph Hitler used the Treaty of Versailles as inspiration to correct what he thought was unfair treatment of the German nation and initiated a second war based on the fascist theory of Aryan superiority.²⁹³

Simultaneously, members of the National Association for the Advancement of Colored People were growing increasingly restless and impatient with the constant terrorist attacks against returning soldiers and Blacks who resisted Jim Crow customs. They turned to one of their executives who was born with such a fair complexion, that he was often mistaken for being Caucasian. Walter White had convinced Du Bois and others in the organization that the best way to expose the atrocities is to investigate the crimes in a clandestine fashion and report the findings in the organization's monthly publication, the *Crisis*. Biographer Thomas Dyja explained the inherent danger: "A black man caught passing in order to spy on whites would be lynched himself."²⁹⁴ White's bravery made him a key figure in the period's political and artistic activism. According to Dyja, "He didn't so much

---

[292] James Weldon Johnson, "The Making of Harlem," *Survey Graphic Magazine* (March, 1925): 635.

[293] Adolph Hitler, *Mein Kampf*, translated by Ralph Manheim (Boston: Houghton Mifflin Company, 1998), 694.

[294] Thomas Dyja, *Walter White: The Dilemma of Black Identity in America* (Chicago: Ivan R. Dee, 2008), 46.

enter the scene that February 1918 as he exploded, initiating nine years of non-stop work that placed him near the center of every sphere of black political, social, and artistic life in the 1920s."[295] White's spirit of activism (though at times placed him at odds with Du Bois, after the latter's return to the NAACP) was essential to the period. It served as an inspiration for his period novel, *Fire on the Flint*.

The New Negro philosophy also inspired a legislative effort to end lynching. In 1925 the NAACP published a full-page advertisement in their *Survey Graphic Magazine*, boasting of White's clandestine efforts to expose and end lynching. Among several points of reference, the publication cited the passage of the Dyer Anti-Lynching Bill. In fact, the House of Representatives passed the legislation, but the bill did not receive enough votes in the Senate. To gain anti-lynching legislation, White testified to Congress recounting his experiences researching terrorist attacks on Blacks in the South. Missouri Representative Leonidas Dyer was impressed and authored the Dyer Anti-Lynching bill. Poignantly, after convincing Dyer of the legislation's necessity, White returned to the South and investigated the lynching of Mary Turner and subsequent murder of her unborn child in Lowndes County, Georgia.[296] He later presented press credentials and secured an audience with Georgia Governor Hugh Dorsey, and anti-lynching supporter, who told White that he was, in fact, powerless to stop the murders. Unfortunately, Southern Democratic senators, through a filibuster maneuver, blocked passage of Dyer's bill.[297] The fact that the United States government was paying reparations to foreign countries whose nationals suffered from the same barbarity while simultaneously refusing to pass the Dyer Anti-Lynching Bill helped fuel the heightened impatience and frustration among Black leaders. In 1905 James Elbert Cutler discussed the American terrorist conundrum as such: "It is a

---

[295] Ibid., 48.
[296] Mary Turner was kidnapped and lynched by a mob. Turner was pregnant, and the trauma of the violent act induced the delivery of a fetus. The mob bludgeoned the newborn to death. Diya discussed the incident in *Walter White: The Dilemma of Black Leadership* (Chicago: Ivan R. Dee, 2008), 51–2.
[297] Ibid.

peculiar situation when the United States can thus be called upon to pay indemnities for lynchings [sic] and yet cannot take steps in several States to prevent their occurrence and cannot in any way hold State governments responsible."[298]

The New Negro reaction that inspired a sense of resistance and determination to defend black lives, was reflected in the works of many of the period's artists. Claude McKay captured the sentiment in his work "If We Must Die." David Levering Lewis surmised that "If We Must Die" gave African Americans a virtual catechism with which to confront the vestiges of the Red Summer of 1919."[299] In lines twelve to fourteen, McKay described the courage, determination, and the decision to resist violence at all costs:

> What though before us lies the open grave?
> Like men we'll face the murderous, cowardly pack,
> Pressed to the wall, dying, but fighting back![300]

The ramifications of racial violence born out the determination of African American war veterans to defend their communities with the same gallantry they displayed in the European war theater were inspiring renewed Black pride. Simultaneously, Louis Armstrong was gallantly sharing his improvisational art with thousands who heard him while employed on a riverboat sailing the Mississippi River from New Orleans to Davenport, Iowa. Thus, his prowess as a jazz and blues musician earned him notoriety beyond his hometown as hundreds would flock to hear the musical approach of his and the boat's band (led by fellow New Orleans musician Fate Marable). For most listeners, it was an introduction to blues music, traditional jazz, and modern dance music, played by the young, but seasoned artist. For Armstrong, it was an opportunity to expand his musical vocabulary and the craft of

---

[298] James Elbert Cutler, *Lynch-Law: An Investigation into the History of Lynching in The United States* (New York: Longmans, Green, and Co., 1905), 260.

[299] David Levering Lewis, *The Portable Harlem Renaissance Reader* (New York: Penguin Books, 1994), 289.

[300] Ibid.

reading music, beyond what he learned in New Orleans at the Colored Waifs Home some eight years earlier. He explained the inspiration, "But I wanted to do more than fake music all the time because there is more to music than playing one style. I lost no time in joining the orchestra on the *Sidney*."[301] Although Armstrong and others may not have been consciously participating in the social revolution that was the summer of 1919, he, like the itinerant blues artists, was spreading a relatively revolutionary musical approach and expounding an American folk art.

Armstrong's contemporaneous connection to the New Negro attitude was partly fueled by the life-long lessons taught to him by Captain Jones. Researcher George Kay surmised, "It was Captain Jones who first taught Louis to blow the bugle." Kay explained further, "But Louis received much more than a musical education at the Waifs' Home. Under the kind parental guidance of Joseph Jones, he acquired a personal dignity and strength of character that remained with him throughout his life."[302] His experiences with Captain and Mrs. Jones, as well as bandmaster Peter Davis, certainly helped forge his mental makeup and approach to life. Also ingrained in the artist were virtues such as trustworthiness, good citizenship, and honesty by his mother, May Ann.

Violent pre-WWI reactions to Black progress were common-place in America, and Armstrong could not escape it, literally. One need only look at the reaction to the rise of the first African American heavyweight boxing champion, Jack Johnson, to see vestiges of the New Negro spirit and attitude. A young Louis Armstrong experienced such reaction during the days after the boxer Jack Johnson became the first Black heavyweight champion, an event that proved seminal in the movement's history. To the chagrin of many whites, Johnson soundly defeated the outmatched Jefferies, knocking him out in the fifteenth round. Many observers thought Johnson, who battered and verbally taunted Jefferies and his corner, could have ended the fight much earlier. In the days following

---

[301] Louis Armstrong, *Satchmo*, 182.
[302] George W. Kay, Foreword, "Louis Armstrong's Letter to His Daddy" *The Second Line, Bicentennial Issue*, 1976, 13–14.

the match, many white Americans retaliated against Black citizens who displayed any racial pride and satisfaction with the fight's outcome. In some cases, they randomly murdered Blacks who were merely going about their daily lives. New Orleans and young Louis Armstrong did not escape the tense atmosphere when he was forced to hide as a gang of whites attacked and beat several Blacks. Biographer Thomas Brothers noted, "Johnson's victory caused white rioting throughout the country and New Orleans was no exception. Armstrong remembered hiding in his house while gangs wandered through the neighborhood in search of random targets on whom to release their rage. Such was the New Orleans into Louis was born."[303] Armstrong recalled,

> That day I was going to get my supply of papers from Charlie, who employed a good many of colored boys like myself. On Canal Street I saw a crowd of colored boys running like mad toward me. I asked one of them what happened. "You better get started, black boy," he said breathlessly as he started to pull me along. 'Jack Johnson just knocked out Jim Jefferies. The white boys are sore about it and they are going to take it out on us.' He did not have to do any urging. I lit out and passed the other boys in a flash. I was a fast runner and when the other boys reached our neighborhood I was at home looking calmly out the window. The next day the excitement had blown over.[304]

Indeed, Black Americans viewed the showdown between Johnson and Jefferies as an opportunity to finally prove their equality in terms of intellectual skills particularly as it relates to athleticism. Booker T. Washington installed a telegraph machine in his residence at Tuskegee Institute to get round-by-round summaries.

Violent terrorist reactions to Black American progress were born out of the myth of the African diaspora's biological inferiority was ingrained

---

[303] Thomas Brothers, *Louis Armstrong's New Orleans*, 14–15.
[304] Armstrong, *Satchmo*, 36.

in American culture. Most Black Americans were either cognizant of Dr. Charles Caldwell's 1835 theory that Blacks are closer on the chain of evolution to apes and monkeys as opposed to Cro-Magnon man or suffered from a lack of social or educational standing because of that belief system. The theory of African or racial inferiority became a mainstay in academia for well into the twentieth century. Dr. Caldwell and others postulated that Blacks indeed did not possess an intellectual capability equal to whites; thus, enslavement and manual labor were not only justified but necessary.[305] Locke described the apparent new attitude among many Black Americans: "...because the Old Negro had long become more of a myth than a man. The Old Negro we must remember, was a creature of moral debate and historical controversy."[306] Locke captured the growing sentiment among African Americans that their worth as citizens and contributors to the American fabric was proven. The explosion of artistic activity, the nation's refusal to pass antiterrorism legislation, as well as an increased awareness of Africa's contribution to world history, helped inspire many to advocate for change to the methodology heretofore used attain social justice. The summer 1919 race riots were a clear indicator that there was indeed a new order. The mob violence Armstrong described is indicative of the terrorist acts that New Negro activists and antilynching proponents Ida B. Wells and White were investigating. Wells used her voice and talents as a journalist to shed light on the anarchy. While Langston Hughes and W.E.B. Du Bois encouraged Black American artists to embrace their gifts and do the same.

In separate spheres, jazz and blues music was coming of age in New Orleans when Wells began exposing the terrorist acts after personal friends of hers were murdered in Memphis. She found that most lynching and terrorist behaviors were from false accusations of a sexual assault against white women by Black men. According to researcher Mia Ba, "Wells' suspicions were confirmed when she began researching every lynching that she read about. What happened in Memphis was not

---

[305] Dr. Charles Caldwell, *Introductory Address on Independence of Intellect*, 1825, 11.
[306] Ibid., 631.

unusual, she found: fully two thirds of victims of lynch mobs were never even accused of rape."[307] Wells's actions as an agent of change continued into the early decades of the twentieth century. Her activism is as indicative of the New Negro spirit as any other. She actively defended Black soldiers falsely accused postwar crimes and participated in the Niagara Movement, which was the precursor to the NAACP, and she was one of a few African American women in the suffrage movement.

The violence and terrorist attacks by many whites were inspired by the more than century-old deliberate dissemination of misinformation about the inhumane system of enslaving Africans. Their belief system in this regard partly embraced an ideology that European colonization of the western hemisphere was a divine endowment and that Blacks lacked humanity and were biologically inferior, thus needing childlike nurturing. More importantly, and pertinent to the roots of much of the terrorist attacks on African Americans, if left unprotected, white females were at risk of suffering sexual assaults by uncontrolled (free) Black men. When considering the native homeland of the enslaved, many, including well-meaning abolitionists, believed that even though the system was indeed cruel, Africa was underdeveloped, devoid of any organized religious order, has no written history, and its inhabitants exist with mores or folkways that encourage uncivilized behaviors. In their opinion, the absence of the desire and/or an ability to do the necessary things (study, practice, and research) was genetic with African Americans.[308] The bigoted belief system was far-reaching. Carter G. Woodson discussed the manifestation of the biased and bigoted apparatus in American education. He isolated science, language, fine arts, literature, and history. With regards to the latter, Woodson surmised:

> In history, of course, the Negro had no place in this curriculum. He was pictured as a human being of lower

---

[307] Mia Bay, Forward to *The Light of Truth: Writings of an Anti-Lynching Crusader*, Ida B. Wells, ed. Mia Bay, Gen Ed. Henty Louis Gates Jr (New York: Penguin Books, 2008).

[308] See James C. King's *The Biology of Race* (Los Angeles: University of California Press 1981), 71–8.

order, unable to subject passion to reason, and therefore useful only when made the hewer of wood and the drawer of water for others. No thought was given to the history of Africa except so far as it had been a field of exploitation for the Caucasian. You might study the history as it was offered in our system elementary school throughout the university, and you would never hear Africa mentioned except in the negative.[309]

Historian Chancellor Williams explored colonialism and slavery as precursors to the minimalization of Africa's and its diaspora's truthful role in world history. "The way was now open and easy for all the relevant branches of science and scholarship to proclaim theories on the inherent inferiority of Blacks."[310] Euro centric writers and many in academia chose to ignore the fact that W. E. B. Du Bois had already published his landmark group of essays, *The Souls of Black Folk*; George W. Carver was on the cusp of revolutionizing farming technology in the South, and new American music called jazz was developing in New Orleans. For many who controlled the textbooks and historical data, it was unfathomable that an art form that incidentally incorporated elements from West Africa, the Caribbean islands, and Europe could come from the creative minds of Charles "Buddy" Bolden, Joe "King" Oliver, Freddie Keppard, and other New Orleans African American performing artists.[311]

Ironically, the transition of this music to the American psyche was made possible because of nearly seventy years of nineteenth-century minstrelsy. This early American music genre dehumanized African Americans promulgating the false theory that enslavement slavery generated a welcome existence, rescuing Blacks from "dark" Africa. In the 1925 publication, the *New Negro*, Locke acknowledged the vestiges as such, and the existential relief apparent during the years leading to and during the period considered here:

---

[309] Carter G. Woodson, *The Mis-Education of the Negro*, 13–4.
[310] Chancellor Williams, *The Destruction of Black Civilization: Great Issues of Race From 4500 B.C. To 2000 A.D* (Chicago, Third World Press,1987) 154.
[311] See Donald Marquis's, *In Search of Buddy Bolden*, 29–39.

> By shedding the old chrysalis of the Negro problem, we are achieving something like a spiritual emancipation. Until recently, lacking self-understanding, we have been almost as much of a problem to ourselves as we still are to others. But the decade that found us with a problem has left us with a task. The multitude perhaps feels as yet only a strange relief and a new vague urge, but the thinking few know that in the reaction the vital inner grip of prejudice has been broken.[312]

Indeed, the performing, literary, and visual arts movement that is the Harlem Renaissance was as Locke described, "a spiritual emancipation." The period's artists were aware of minstrelsy's stereotypes, and they creatively attempted to contrast those heretofore artistic norms in their respective mediums.

In the context of the *New Negro* discussion here, the Du Bois and Locke perspectives regarding the arts are relative. Harlem Renaissance artists faced creative impediments to their productions of art representative of Black America, and as discussed in a previous chapter, Du Bois thought art needed to serve as propaganda for the good of the Black community.[313][314] Indeed, he openly questioned and challenged the role of white critics who chose to define, thus deciding what is good or bad in Black American culture. He understood the inherent and apparent pitfalls when one group sets the standards and parameters for another's culture. Notably, in the context of what is right or wrong. The decision of whether to follow creative instincts or adhere to patron/benefactor aesthetics was often challenging to make. When discussing the situation confronting African American artists, Locke acknowledged the problem as such:

> His shadow, so to speak has been more real to him than his personality. Through having had to appeal from

---

[312] Alain Locke, The New Negro, ed. Alain Locke in *The New Negro* (New York: Atheneum Publishers, 1925), 5.
[313] See Du Bois's 1926 speech, "The Criteria of Negro Art," 15.

the unjust stereotypes of his oppressors and traducers to those of his liberators, friends and benefactors he has had to subscribe to the traditional positions from which his case has been viewed. Little true social or self-understanding has or could come from such a situation.[314]

Locke's assessment encapsulated the inherent dilemma for Black artists. Armstrong overcame the dilemma with the help of mentor Joe "King" Oliver. Indeed, one can argue that Oliver's spirit of entrepreneurship was juxtaposed with artistic exploration are vestiges of the New Negro sentiment.

Armstrong seemed to have ignored any attempts (if indeed there were any) to interfere with his artistic development. His creative trajectory accelerated as his career rose steadily. His 1920 arrival in Chicago for what turned out to be a two-year engagement with King Oliver's band affirmed the latter's continuing inspiration on the young artist's improvisational choices. According to Thomas Brothers, "Armstrong's main musical debt to Oliver must have been in details of improvisational style, especially in up-tempo 'ragtime'… These attributes that Armstrong would credit to Oliver would also sum up Armstrong's special stylistic qualities."[315] The immediate and collective musical improvisation in a traditional New Orleans jazz ensemble was on display nightly in Chicago venues like the Vendome. "King" Oliver became not only his mentor and a father figure, but also a musical guru helping to transform Armstrong into a virtuoso protégé. Indeed, the group's augmented instrumentation (duo cornets) allowed Armstrong to explore the expansion of the traditional roles established in the wind instruments of an early New Orleans jazz ensemble. Armstrong's deep admiration for Oliver, both personally and musically, allowed for nightly musical creations that reached new heights in the context of

---

[314] Nathan W. Huggins, "Visual Arts: To Celebrate Blackness," *Voices from the Harlem Renaissance* (New York: Oxford University Press, 1995), 47.

[315] Thomas Brothers ed., *Louis Armstrong: In His Own Words, Selected Writings* (New York: Oxford University Press, 1999) 37.

the New Orleans brass band style of collective improvisation. Later, in recordings such as "Texas Moaner Blues," Armstrong would assume the role of the clarinetist (embellish the melody) in a traditional brass band setting when he musically responded to Irvis's and Bechet's improvisational ventures.[316] His familiarity with the blues, juxtaposed with a degree of technical ability that included being able in a relatively high trumpet and cornet pitch range (notes C and D) sometimes fifty times consecutively. This is still considered in the upper range of the trumpet, made him an instant hit in Chicago.[317]

Armstrong's improvisational prowess shifted the focus in jazz music to the creative talents of a single artist. His choices displayed a rhythmic "swing" that was to become imitated in a variety of American musical genres for the rest of the twentieth century. Armstrong's style of swing is his invention and an outgrowth of all the traditional jazz heard as he was coming of age in New Orleans, including Freddie Keppard, "Big Eyed" Louis Nelson, and Bunk Johnson, among others. His improvisational choices were on display for all to hear in his earliest recordings like "Chimes Blues." Analytically, his choices in the twelve-bar blues song context are indicative of a seasoned musician who understands the blues music and the role(s) of the accompanying instruments.[318] Interestingly, Locke thought the period's literary, visual, and performing arts were the result of a necessity to embrace a relatively new atmosphere of unfettered artistic freedom: "It was rather the necessity for fuller, truer self-expression, the realization of the unwisdom [sic] of allowing social discrimination to segregate him mentally. And a counter attitude to cramp and fetter his own living—and so the 'spite-wall' that the intellectuals built over the color line has happily been taken down."[319] Armstrong's improvisational art was the height of "fuller, more authentic self-expression" that incredibly inspired the

---

[316] Sidney Bechet explores the musical role of the clarinetist in early New Orleans jazz in his autobiography, *Treat It Gentle*, 77–94.

[317] See Teachout's biography, *Pops: A Life of Louis Armstrong*, 51–79.

[318] The 1923 recording session that included *Chime Blues* was Armstrong's first studio experience.

[319] Ibid., 632.

oppressor to imitate the oppressed. Armstrong's truer 'self-expression' wasn't happenstance, but born out of his New Orleans experiences.

The *New Negro* sentiment was present in many of the eductional institutions in the African American community, and Louis Armstrong benefited from such training. Schools such as Fisk College, Albany Bible and Manual Training Institute, and Clark College, among others, were producing teachers, musicians, artists, nurses, and medical-and dental-school candidates. Evidence of the infinite possibilities and verification of Dubois's philosophy was present in Washington's creation, Tuskegee Institute. Tuskegee professor and former enslaved, George Washington Carver was exploring the possibilities available in Southern peanut, soybean, and cotton crops. He and his students' curiosity produced hundreds of ways of uses, including soy products, paint, axle grease, genetic research, and massage oil, which proved helpful to those stricken with polio. The early visual artist turned botanist helped pioneer the chemurgy field. According to researcher Helga Schier, "In addition to focusing on the nutritional value of foods, Carver worked for decades of turning agriculture raw materials into industrial products."[320] Carver's philosophy of no excuses, clean living, and diligence mirrored his employer, Booker T. Washington. The fruits of his research are, to this very day, enjoyed the world over. Institutions such as Tuskegee and the Albany Bible and Manual Institute promoted racial pride and no excuses while striving for excellence. The Colored Waifs

Meta Warrick Fuller (Schomburg Center, New York Public Library)

Archibald Motley (Schomburg Center, New York Public Library)

---

[320] Helga Schier, *George Washington Carver: Agricultural Innovator* (Edina, Minnesota: ABDO Publishing Co, 2008) 48.

Home for Boys, where Armstrong received heretofore unfamiliar institutional discipline, was no exception. Educators were, for the most part, graduates of segregated colleges and universities or "Historically Black Colleges and Universities."[321] Armstrong's teachers were graduates of New Orleans Straight School (a teacher training institute), which is now Dillard University. Researcher Will Buckingham discussed the significance of the school's vocal music teacher, Naomi Spriggins (an alumnus of New Orleans Straight School) "who gave Louis Armstrong his first 'singing lessons' during his stint at the Colored Waifs Home for Boys."[322]

Not surprisingly, many of the period's visual artists embraced the New Negro attitude and its philosophical fervor. Indeed, they and the literary and performing artists were cognizant of the war efforts, antilynching sentiments, and constitutional rights. In separate camps and various mediums, Aaron Douglas, Archibald Motley Jr., Paul Van der Zee, and Meta Warrick-Fuller painted, photographed, and carved vestiges of Black life and cultural behavior. For example, Motley Jr.'s creation, *The Blues*, captures on canvas a crowded dance floor similar to the one described by Duke Ellington in his composition "Don't Get Around Much Anymore" and Fats Waller's "This Joint Is Jumping."[323] Both pieces define party venues that were commonplace in Harlem with crowds that are indicative of a nightly party atmosphere. Warrick-Fuller produced works as a sculptor

Ethiopia Awakening
(Schomburg Center,
New York Public Library)

---

[321] Dr. Joseph Holley detailed the challenges of recruiting qualified teachers in rural Georgia in his autobiography, *You Can't Build a Chimney from the Top*, 53–80.

[322] Will Buckingham, "Louis Armstrong and the Waif's Home," *The Jazz Archives*, XXIV (2011): 7.

[323] The texts of Ellington's *Don't Get Around Much Anymore*, and Waller's *This Joint Is Jumping* describes in detail a "speakeasy" dance and lounge venue typical in the Harlem community during the era considered here.

that captured the serious side of life in Harlem. *Ethiopia Awakening* and *Dark Hero* were two of her more famous works. Paul Van Der Zee's photography gives the viewer a sense of the depth of the neighborhood's upper and middle class. Importantly, Aaron Douglas's visual artworks capture the area's mood, and resulting cultural behaviors. It also codified the inspiration (apparent in these artists) to express the aesthetics of the cultural behaviors in a relative medium.

Langston Hughes, Charles Johnson, E. Franklin Frazier, Rudolf Fisher, and Hubert Delaney (Schomburg Center, New York Public Library)

Collaborations between some visual and literary artists took place at the behest of publications such as the *Survey Graphic, Crisis,* and *Opportunity* magazines. For example, after reading Georgia Johnson's poem, called "The Black Runner," Aaron Douglas illustrated a work depicting the efforts of a half-clad runner in full stride. Amy Kirschke discussed Douglas's disappointment with the work despite Johnson's approval: "Douglas originally thought his work was 'pretty good' but then became dissatisfied with it. He was surprised when Johnson wrote him thanking for the drawing."[324] The party life in Harlem was an indelible part of the artist's choices. For example, *To Midnight Nan*

---

[324] Amy Kirschke, *Aaron Douglas: Art, Race and the Harlem Renaissance* (Jackson: The University of Mississippi Press, 1995), 71.

at Leroy is an illustration of two people enjoying each other through the medium of dance, fueled by jazz music in a nightclub setting. His interest in ancient African visual arts inspired *Invincible Music, the Spirit of Africa*. Kirschke surmised, "Here Egypt represents Africa. Douglas was trying to simplify the human form.

Two shield like marquis shapes are implanted in the ground behind the figure, with jagged design on them that resembles African-inspired patterning."[325] Former Douglas student and twentieth-century artist Dr. Arthur Berry discussed Douglas's ability to recognize the creativity in his contemporaries such as Pablo Picasso: "The other thing was, I said to him was that stuff about back then, Picasso paintings and so forth and how he was the master, he (Douglass) could see everybody else, he could look at his (Picasso) paintings and see he used the work of many other artists."[326] Douglas's choice to embrace African American themes in his creations placed him in the canon of the period's visual artists. Critics who argue the validity of the Harlem Renaissance visual arts readily point to Douglas's art as an example of an embracing of African American culture.

Images in the performing, literary, and visual arts mediums often ignited or contributed to the debate regarding the purpose of the period's arts. To this end, the militancy inspired by the New Negro sentiments forced artists to look inward when contemplating theirs and other African American cultural contributions. Deeper still were the consumer expectations and their impact upon art. Such expectations shaped the artist's choices. Earlier, Paul Lawrence Dunbar chose to use the slave dialect to gain acceptance from a wider audience. He expressed disappointment with the fact that the demand for his dialect-based poems did not allow him to create more works in standard English. Researcher Charles Johnson discussed Dunbar's dilemma at a conference organized to explore the uniqueness of the Harlem Renaissance: "But in his candid moments, Dunbar confessed to Johnson (James Weldon Johnson) that he resorted to dialect verse to gain a hearing and then nothing but his dialect verse would be accepted. He never got to the

---

[325] Ibid., 76.
[326] Dr. Arthur Berry interview by author, Albany, GA, 10/22/2012.

things he really wanted to do."³²⁷ Dunbar's struggle is not unlike other artists who despite new art, the consumer insists on old art.

Similarly, and by choice, Armstrong's stage presence was an integral part of his performing art.³²⁸ He successfully traversed the dynamic between artist and consumer by making many who may otherwise oppress him feel a level of comfort as a receiver and accepting of his art. Many consumers of his music were comfortable with his artistic prowess but drew the line with full enfranchisement or equal education and living opportunities under the edict of the Plessey versus Ferguson "separate but equal" ruling. Whether with the Joe "King" Oliver Creole Band in Chicago, the Fletcher Henderson Orchestra in New York, or his own Hot Five and Hot Seven groups, Armstrong's art pushed the genre from an ensemble-focused aggregation concerned primarily with a collective group effort to an emphasis upon the individual soloist. Unlike Paul Lawrence Dunbar, he felt readily free to create the art of his choice through virtuosic instrumental performance and vocal means.

Historic parallels to systemic racism are clear when one understands that approximately one hundred years before Dunbar's exploits and the Harlem Renaissance, American actor Thomas D. Rice encountered an enslaved stable hand in Kentucky who, like many others, produced art that functioned as a vehicle to help get a laborious task done as well as gain a melancholy relief. Rice, from an outsider's perspective, attempted to recreate the laborer's functional art in the context of a concert stage. He called his caricature "Jim Crow," which was the name of the song he heard being sung by the laborer. Subsequently, Rice and other "Ethiopian Delineators" perpetuated the false image of the enslaved as happy laborers. To many, Armstrong's stage mannerisms were a throwback to minstrel stage caricatures. His stage presence personified a musician that was happy to share his art. Unfortunately,

---

[327] Charles Johnson, "The Negro Renaissance and its Significance," *The New Negro Thirty Years Afterward* (Washington, DC: Howard University Press, 1955), 208.

[328] Much of the criticism of Armstrong was of his stage presence that reminded many of the minstrel characters that predominated American culture during the previous century.

it was reminiscent of some racist stereotypes perpetuated in American music on the nineteenth-century minstrel stage.[329]

Specifically, Frederick Douglass discussed the premise of a happy slave: "The remark is not unfrequently made, that slaves are the most contented and happy laborers in the world. They dance and sing, and make all manner of joyful noises—so they do; but it is a great mistake to suppose them happy because they sing."[330] Armstrong's ever-present smile on stage reminded some of the Rice's and others' black-faced stage creations, or at the least, variations of those caricatures.

Significant to historical and cultural importance of Armstrong is the fact that his stage demeanor successfully made his listeners relaxed as they anticipated the pleasure of being entertained by one of the nation's early jazz and blues music masters. More often than not, a transformation or cultural awakening happens when the consumer considers or reconsiders the humanity of a people who possessed the propensity to create such an art. The receiver unconsciously discards what social scientist Joy DeGruy-Leary and others call a "cognitive dissonance."[331] The human instinct Dr. Leary identified arises when one becomes aware of and empathizes with a group suffering mistreatments such as lynching, terrorism, or genocide. Some choose to rectify the existence of such treatment by ridding themselves of cognitive dissonance. Degruy-Leary believed the process of dehumanization is a coping method for the uncomfortable instinct or "cognitive dissonance" that arises upon an awareness of acts of inhumanity: "Humans do not particularly like this discomfort so whenever it occurs we almost immediately try to resolve it. And we can resolve it in one of two ways. One way is to own up to the negative act and address the harm caused by it. The other way is to justify the negative act rather than admit to

---

[329] See Ken Burns's Documentary, *Jazz: Episode Three, Our Language* Musicologists discuss the misgivings many Black musicians and consumers had with Armstrong's stage presence.

[330] Eileen Southern, *Readings in Black American Music*, (New York: W. W. Norton and Co., 1983), 84.

[331] Joy Degruy-Leary, *The Post Traumatic Slave Syndrome* (Milwaukie, Oregon: Uptone Press, 2005), 54.

the wrongdoing. 'They deserve it,' is a typical justification"³³² Degruy-Leary's theory places into context the thought process of consumers who assessed (or reassessed) their prejudices about the people that created the music. In other instances, the music inspired resistance to tyranny and fascism.

One of the unintended consequences beyond the period considered here was Armstrong's and American jazz's European tours was the inspiration to organize the underground resistance to German fascism by the French anti-Nazi movement.³³³ French freedom fighters organized clandestine intimate jazz performances after Nazi forces occupied Western Europe and banned the music. To this end, Armstrong and other touring American jazz (Harlem Renaissance) artists may have inspired some concertgoers to regain their cognitive dissonance. Armstrong's and other's audiences more than likely were familiar with the violence perpetrated on the descendants of African enslaved and the vestiges of colonialism on the African continent. Additionally, the contributions of other period musicians such as Sidney Bechet, Duke Ellington, Noble Sissle, Eubie Blake, and Will Marion Cook, who successfully toured most of Europe, Turkey, and the Soviet Union before World War II are equally important. French writer and filmmaker Bertrand Tavernier surmised, "It (jazz) was a way of fighting against the conformists, fighting against the spirit of fascists, fighting against the German atmosphere. It was a symbol of resistance; not only because it was American, but it was music created by blacks, and that was important when you are fighting against a racist government."³³⁴ Tavernier affirms the power of jazz (and its precursor, blues music) as a transformative and inspirational art that inspires the same resistance to oppression by the victims of fascism in Europe and racism in America. What is of significant note here is that in the post–World War I and

---

[332] Ibid., 54.

[333] Stefan Grapelli, jazz musician and member of the Anti-Nazi French Resistance Movement, described the group's inspiration for resisting Nazi fascism from the music of Louis Armstrong.

[334] Bertrand Tavernier, *Jazz: A Film by Ken Burns* (Episode Seven, *Dedicated to Chaos*, Alexandria, VA: 2000).

pre–World War II European context, listeners who heard Armstrong, Ellington, Bechet, and others would have been forced to challenge, on one hand, the moral and political validity of colonialism in Africa and other parts of the world. Additionally, the receivers of Armstrong's art may have been considering the humanity of African Americans and the humanity of those who were (at the time of Armstrong's tour) victims of the fascist ideologies of Adolph Hitler.

The Harlem Renaissance's rise and fall were not proportionate, though the latter was predictable after the 1929 stock market crash. Though the rise regarding the quantity (when placed in this context) and popularity was relatively quick, the fall was even faster after 1930. The period may have depended too much on philanthropic cognitive dissonance and the continued consumption of blues music. Indeed, Harlem Renaissance's rapid demise mirrors the nation's economic downfall after the 1929 stock market crash. Benefactors became increasingly unable or unwilling to support not only American arts in general, but also African American period arts. By the end of the new century's third decade, blues music was indeed an integral entity in American pop culture.[335] Insiders and outsiders saturated the market with creations, and many the outsiders considered themselves legitimate artists and experts of Black cultural life. Indeed, the canon of work produced by Tin Pan Alley songwriters such as George Gershwin and Irving Berlin were evident in a frenzy associated with the monies generated by the music's popularity.

Another contributing factor was the propensity of some artists to record and rerecord under pseudo names. One can see the evidence of this in a letter written by W. C. Handy to his client Arthur Neal explaining the reasons for declining revenues. In a 1929 (prestock market crash) correspondence to a frustrated Neale, Handy partially explained why the artist's blues song has not garnered success: "Everything we put out last year was a flop. It's not because they aren't good songs. It is because the game is becoming tighter and tighter each year, and a song is only what you are able to make it. Men can sit up over a bottle of liquor and a meal and cigar, and plan a dozen hits and put them

---

[335] See Elijah Wald's *Escaping the Delta: Robert Johnson and the Invention of the Blues* (New York: Harper Collins Books, 2004), 1–13.

over"[336] Handy expressed his and other Black American blues artists' frustration with the temerity of many who would sacrifice the quality and authenticity of the art to generate revenue.

The worldwide economic crisis following the 1929 stock market crash affected artists' careers to varying degrees. Consumer expectations and satisfaction allowed the artists to have a level of creativity and fiscal stability, even during the trying early years of depression. Zora Neal Hurston, for example, continued to research and publish in the fictional medium. Her stories ("Mules and Men" and "Their Eyes Were Watching God") told of Black life and the impact of music in the rural South.[337] Meanwhile, Armstrong and his Hot Seven Orchestra took advantage of a fertile alternative market and made a triumphant tour of Europe. The tour included a concert in Holland that was audio and visually recorded. The audience in Holland, like all the other tour stops, experienced Armstrong's artistry and mastery of the American art form presented with the unique Armstrong style that makes the listener (via humbled presentation) so comfortable that the listener leaves with an acceptance of the humanity of Africans and African Americans.

The phenomena of art that is created by the oppressed and then consumed and or appropriated by oppressor became the subject or research for cultural theorist Frantz Fanon. The theorist discussed the derogatory nomenclature created by colonizers to justify colonization and the colonized task of processing of redefining the oppressor's propaganda: "The colonized know all that and roar with laughter every time they hear themselves called an animal by the other, for they know they are not animals. And at the very moment when they discover their humanity, they begin to sharpen their weapons to secure its victory."[338] Armstrong's artistic instincts are reflected Fanon's theory. He discovered his humanity during his early years in New Orleans when he learned

---

[336] *William Christopher Handy to Arthur Neale*, February 12, 1919, Houghton Library, Harvard University, Cambridge, MA.

[337] Zora Neal Hurston's *Mules and Men* is a collection of folk tales and songs gathered from anthropological research in the South. *Their Eyes Were Watching God* is one of the writer's seminal fictional works.

[338] Frantz Fanon, *The Wretched of the Earth* (New York: Grove Press, 1963), 8.

the tenants of discipline from school headmaster Captain Jones while learning to play music in an ensemble setting from teacher Peter Davis. His sense of humanity heightened when he learned more about the art of improvisation from Joe "King" Oliver, among others. Some who heard him, whether performing on the riverboat in 1919 or 1935 before the outbreak of World War II, reacquired their cognitive dissonance.

At the risk of being banal or redundant, though the period known as the Harlem Renaissance was relatively brief, it produced some of America's more significant examples of literary, visual, and performing arts and artists. David Levering Lewis reached this conclusion about the period:

> Although the emergence of the Harlem Renaissance seems much more sudden and dramatic in retrospect than the historic reality, its institutional elaboration was, in fact, relatively quick. Because so little fiction or poetry had been produced by African-Americans in the years prior to the Harlem Renaissance, the appearance of a dozen or more poets and novelists and essayists seem all the more striking and improbable.[339]

The interrelationships between the life and music of Louis Armstrong, the period known as the Harlem Renaissance, the popularity of blues music, and the philosophical and political admonitions of the period's seminal figures are tangible. In hindsight, what may appear as unrelated circumstances were historical events that directly influenced the New Negro sentiment. Ida B. Wells's efforts to shed light on terrorism to the world, Jack Johnson's prowess in the ring juxtaposed with his decision to break the taboo of interracial romantic relationships, and the reaction

---

[339] 340 David Levering Lewis, "The Intellectual Luminaries of the Harlem Renaissance," *The Journal of Blacks in Higher Education*, no. 7 (Spring, 1995): 68.

[2] W. E. B. Du Bois's and Booker T. Washington's disagreement can be identified in DuBois's chapter in *Souls of Black Folks* titled On Mr. Washington and Others. In Schuyler's essay, "The Negro Art-Hokum," he loathed the proclivities period's African American art. Hughes retorted with his reply, "The Negro Artist and the Racial Mountain."

of many African American World War I veterans to the maltreatment upon returning home from the war were contributions to the literary, artistic choices at the dawn of the Harlem Renaissance.

In retrospect, Louis Armstrong's art and consequently, one of the period's significant performing art, was a direct result of the mores and folkways present in the culture of his birthplace, New Orleans.

The significance here is that the region's earliest enslaved population was primarily (two-thirds) Senegambians, and all were descendants of the medieval empires of Ghana, Mali, and Songhay. They introduced cultural behaviors, which included a communal approach to making music, the use of polyrhythms, and percussive body usage. Decades later, during the post-Civil War years, the West African's descendants (as well as the descendants of those enslaved from other West African nations) used the same approach to making music when they fused blues and ragtime music. The music that a young Armstrong heard and played (including the sacred music of the area's Black churches) was, in large part, based on the music created by the same descendants. Blues and jazz music arose from the music of the post-enslavement African Americans' aesthetic choices, specifically, field hollers and work songs. The subsequent art was functional as it was music that served to assist with various labor tasks. Similarly, the enslaved created the performing art or spirituals, to covertly send messages of planned escapes to each other.

Blues music's exportation to the North and beyond was not merely coincidental when placed in the context of the *New Negro Movement*. Indeed, the performing art initially took multiple paths. Many of the New Orleans musicians followed their lay brethren and migrated to urban areas in the north, including Chicago and Harlem, or in Freddie Keppard's and "Jelly Roll" Morton's case, west to Los Angeles. Still, other blues musicians maintained their residency in suburban areas of the South and played the music to consuming audiences. Both groups of artists impacted the Harlem Renaissance and, subsequently, American music. The popularity of the genre is evident in the number of record sales, particularly though not exclusively in the Black community. The invention of sound recording and the interest in the uniqueness of Black American folk music inspired growth in the art's popularity. The demand for individual artists in smaller ensemble settings increased through groups like Armstrong's Hot Five and the earlier Fletcher Henderson Orchestra, which featured Louis Armstrong. The latter successfully though not exclusively performed blues music. Seminal blues music artists, Ma Rainey, Bessie Smith, and Ethel Waters, all signed contracts in the "race record" division of recording companies. Armstrong's impact in this setting is significant. I should be restated here that he recorded 114 times as a sideman with dozens of blues artists between 1923 and 1930.

Harlem Renaissance literary artists were not immune to the rise in blues music's popularity. The performing art considered here was the central theme of much of their works. For example, Langston Hughes captured blues music's impact on cultural behaviors in Harlem venues in poems such as "Weary Blues" and "Jazzonia." In both creations, Hughes simultaneously romanticizes the music's power to recognize one's ills and the possible solution(s) available to them. Thus, blues music similarly functions as a liberating force as its precursor did in earlier settings, such as cotton or sugarcane plantations. The early performing art served (functioned) to help the sharecropper/artist cope with the aggregate amount of the tasks at hand. Period literary artist Fenton Johnson also captured in literary prose the impact of blues music in "The Banjo Player." Similarly, Sterling Brown penned an ode to blues music pioneer Ma Rainey with a poem titled "Ma Rainey." Brown expressed in the context of Thomas Dewey's theory Art as Experience, the aesthetic value of hearing blues music from the receiver's perspective.

The importance and significance of blues music in American culture are apparent to the National Aeronautics and Space Administration. On September 5, 1977, NASA launched the Voyager I satellite to probe interstellar space beyond the earth's direct solar system. The organization placed items on board as a contingency in case the spacecraft encountered extraterrestrials. NASA put representations of human experience on planet Earth on the rocket. Among those were examples of music, including a recording by 1920s itinerant blues musician, "Blind" Willie Johnson. The apocryphal story is that the artist was blinded as a child when his stepmother threw lye in his eyes in retaliation for being abused by Johnson's father. Johnson earned a modicum of success as his art, not unlike that of others in the blues genre, captured life's trials and tribulations. Johnson's music often describes the difficulty of navigating existence in the Jim Crow South. He also recorded gospel songs or, more specifically, blues music with sacred texts. Sadly, he died penniless on a cold floor in his home after a fire heavily damaged it. Poignantly, the song NASA chose was recorded fifty years earlier during the Harlem Renaissance and titled "Dark Was the Night, Cold Was the Floor."

The significance of NASA's decision to include Black American folk music recorded during the Harlem Renaissance era is an example of the human experience is infinitely valuable. Performing artist Wynton Marsalis surmised, "To accept the music of the Negro is to accept the humanity of the Negro." Indeed, the period's contributors were not the first artists and activists to tell the story of Black life in America. However, their artistic contributions and the renewed sense of history inspired generations of artists and theorists throughout the twentieth and early twenty-first centuries. Louis Armstrong lived for an additional forty years and contributed significantly to the American music canon. He altered the path of American music even in the face of prejudice and racism as his art still sets the standard for improvisation. In hindsight, what may appear as unrelated circumstances were historical events that directly influenced the New Negro philosophy, political thought, and the literary, visual, and performing arts between 1923 and 1930, known as the Harlem Renaissance. The end of the artistic era explored here (as all other cultural periods) was inevitable. Beyond the stock market crash of 1929, the period's philosophers, theorists, and artists were not able to shift the racial paradigm in place in America since and before the nation's birth. David Levering Lewis opined:

> They knew that not to be white in America was to be something less than human, whatever their valedictorian achievements. They recognized that, by the laws of the South and customs of the North, the fundamental distinction drawn by most white Americans was between good and bad Afro-Americans. In this dehumanized

scheme of things, neither culture nor color could alter the pariah status of those whose ancestors had been African slaves.[340]

Lewis's thoughts reflect the ongoing debate as to the legitimacy of the period. Some contemporary doubters view the period as figments of the white American imagination. Historian John Henrik Clarke thought that the period literary art was "parochial at best." Despite the admonitions of Du Bois, Woodson, Schomburg, Garvey, Hughes, and other scholars, many of the period's white benefactors and consumers were African Americans through a binary lens. Blacks were entertaining but unworthy of access to all that the Constitution guarantees. Indeed, the conscious decision to ignore, misappropriate, eliminate, and create mendacious curricula was a decision to perpetuate the falsehood that the African diaspora are inherently incapable of participation in historical and cultural advancement. Artistic achievements before and after the Harlem Renaissance, military participation, and bravery in every conflict, educational achievement, and economic advancement are marginalized or viewed as aberrations by many of those set policies that govern the lives of all Americans. A careful study of the period and the different and historical factors leading to its existence will enhance help eliminate many of the misconceptions of the Black American experience.

Louis Armstrong
(Louis Armstrong House and Museum)

---

[340] David Levering Lewis, *When Harlem Was In Vogue*, 305.

CHAPTER VII

CODA

Louis Armstrong's artistic choices both instrumentally and vocally between 1923 and 1930 influenced the evolution of African-American literary, visual, and performance arts. Armstrong's impact on the popularity of American blues music both directly and indirectly played a part in the philosophical, artistic, and political choices during the period considered here. Though relatively early in his life-journey, one can hear signs of artistic manifestations born out of his existential experiences growing up in New Orleans in the 1924 collaboration with fellow period contributor, Sidney Bechet. The two joined period entrepreneur and impresario Clarence Williams and recorded the latter's composition, *Texas Moaner Blues*. It was, in fact, Armstrong's second published recording session. In 1923 he recorded several sides as a member of Joe "King" Oliver's Original Creole Jazz Band including the seminal *Chimes Blues*.

Indeed, an analysis of the music transcription of (*Texas Moaner Blues*) the ensemble's wind instruments (see Figure 2 in Chapter I) reveals two New Orleans musicians steeped in the blues tradition. Though they are relatively early in their careers, both possess the performing instincts of seasoned blues music professionals. Notably, Armstrong's improvisational stop-time exploration suggests an early bebop style, though that genre was not on the scene for another sixteen years. He simultaneously mirrored earlier New Orleans jazz musicians while shifting the focus of the performing art to individual improvisational in the context of the blues music. His artistic choices were so impactful during the Harlem Renaissance that they permanently changed the landscape of American music throughout the remainder of the twentieth century. One can identify vestiges of the earlier West African musical practices decades earlier in Armstrong's place of birth, New Orleans' Congo Square. Similarly, musicians were expected to improvise in the context of the song. The mores and folkways present in New Orleans and during Armstrong's childhood and adolescent years inspired his musical instincts.

The rise in Armstrong's popularity as a performing artist parallels the trajectory of blues music's popularity from 1924 through 1930. However, critics of the Harlem Renaissance either did not recognize or underestimated Armstrong's contributions to the period and the subsequent impact on black American cultural pride during the period considered here. Often, their African-American and African-centric choices resulted in positive implications. The artists did not want to exist in alterity with the African diaspora. Activist Franz Fanon explained, "The blacks who lived in the United States, Latin, and Central America needed a cultural matrix to cling to."[341] Langston Hughes said black artists have a plethora of subjects available to them "Without going outside his race, and even among the better classes with their 'white' culture and conscious American manners, but still Negro enough to be different, there is sufficient matter to furnish a black artist with a lifetime of creative work."[342] Armstrong's role here is of significance. During the Harlem Renaissance, he inspired a change in the communal (musicians and consumers) aesthetics. Artistically, he created an atmosphere that shifted the focus of jazz and blues music (in an ensemble setting) from an emphasis on the collective polyphony to one of individuality inherent in an artist's improvisational skills. Musical options that are improvised instantly in a performance setting

---

[341] Franz Fanon, *The Wretched of the Earth* (New York: Grove Press, 1963), 153.

[342] Langston Hughes, "The Negro Artist and the Racial Mountain," *The Nation* CXXII (June 1926): 692-94.

became the basis for jazz music and consequently the artistic choices of Armstrong. Though his career spanned most of the twentieth century, it is the context of his creativity during the Harlem Renaissance that is the focus of this research.

Additionally, blues music's rise in popularity between 1923 and 1930 was significantly due to Armstrong's influence on the period's performing artists. They include the likes of Ethel Waters, Mamie Smith, and Bessie Smith (often with Armstrong's accompaniment) helped fuel an increase in the popularity of blues music and subsequently the themes of much of the literary and visual art. The music's presence as an integral part of many black American lives is evident in poems of literary artists Langston Hughes, Fenton Johnson, and Sterling Brown. Collectively, they wrote some of the period's most important and critically acclaimed works with the production of blues music as the focal point. *Weary Blues, Banjo Player*, and *Ode to Ma Rainey* are three notable examples of such works. Period visual artists, Aaron Douglass's *Play de Blues* and Archibald Motley, Jr.'s, *Blues* are examples of works with blues music as its text. They creatively resisted many of the accepted academic practices and instinctively used the genre's performance settings (nightclubs, rent parties) as their subjects or central themes. The artists were cognizant of the music's ability to make urban life bearable for the consumer while recalling the music's same function to those who were familiar with it in its original rural Southern setting.

The philosophical underpinnings that drove the consciousness of many of the period's social theorists were influenced (though indirectly) by Armstrong's art and blues music's popularity. Indeed, simultaneous to Armstrong's salient artistic choices and the rise in the music's popularity, a debate arose as to the purpose of the period's art. Some, such as W.E.B. Du Bois believed that Black American art is potentially a useful tool for propaganda. The sociologist and co-founder of the National Association for the Advancement of Colored People advocated for the exposure, through the arts, of the oppressive laws, of terrorist activities (lynching) and social injustices that were the African-American experience. Du Bois and many African-American leaders held a heightened disappointment with the failure of the American government to recognize the bravery and patriotism shown by black American soldiers during World War I. Du Bois's disappointment was exponentially increased when he learned of the United States government's directive to their French counterparts not to promote fraternization between the black troops and white citizens. The fear was that the Black American war veterans would expect the same social treatment when they return home. Historically, they fought valiantly and were highly decorated by the French government. It is also of significant note that Du Bois's concern for the future of colonialism was heightened when the proposed peace plan at the Paris Conference evolved into an expansion of imperialism rather than an opportunity for independence on the African continent. He (Du Bois) chose to encourage black artists to create works that challenged the societal norms which perpetuated the oppression, disenfranchisement, black codes, terrorism, and suffocating economic conditions that overwhelmed the African-American community indeed, the same conditions that inspired the creation of blues music.

In 1926, Du Bois detailed his views to an unsuspecting audience in a keynote address to the NAACP, titled *The Criteria of Negro Art*. Conversely, in his 1928 essay *Art or Propaganda*, Alain Locke expressed his belief that the best way to achieve multi-cultural acceptance in America would be for African-American art to acquiesce to European (Western) standards. The cultural critic and theorist believed that if an artist solely used Black American concerns as their themes, it would be an admittance of a collective lack of intellect or inability to meet established Euro-centric standards. The debate's crescendo paralleled the rise in popularity of blues music, and by 1928, record sales and sales of sheet music verified the performing art's transformation into an integral part of the nation's popular culture.

Many of the period's critics agreed with Locke's point with regards to the purpose of black art. However, the influence of the increasing philanthropic support concerned both sides of the debate. Locke openly sought monetary support from well-meaning individuals who were interested in promoting black American literary and visual art. Indeed, most of the social organizations including Du Bois's NAACP welcomed such support. However, some, particularly those in academia like Joseph W. Holley, founder of the Albany Bible and Manual Training Institute, was primarily concerned with being accepted by a Western-based educational infrastructure that did not regard African-American art as worthy of scholarly review. Consequently, adopting the works of Hughes, Armstrong, or Douglass into the canon of American art was outside of the curriculum possibilities. David Levering Lewis explained the post-World War I efforts to fund higher education, especially the private black schools: "Harvard and Columbia having been secured, the battle for Atlanta, Fisk, Howard, and Lincoln was launched in the mid-twenties. Atlanta University was destined to be 'saved' by the General Education Board plan to make it a graduate institution serviced by local colleges with academic and service programs more in tune with white southern philosophy."[343] Despite the creativity heard in Armstrong's recordings and live performances, many in academia developed a disdain for African-American arts and considered the area unqualified for scholarly research and discussion. Most of the African Americans who held similar opinions as to the purpose and place and role of black arts agreed with Booker T. Washington's theory of accommodation. Indeed, their philosophical and political beliefs were precursors to present-day black conservatism.

One of the period's most outspoken black critics was the black conservative satirist and cultural critic, and Booker T. Washington devotee, George Schuyler, himself a veteran of the 360th regiment. His essay, *The Negro Art-Hokum* is seminal to the black conservative construct particularly in the context of African-American and Harlem Renaissance arts. In the essay, Schuyler questioned the validity and quality of the period's African-American arts. Schuyler explained, "As for the literature, painting, and sculptor of Aframericans---such as there is—it is identical in kind with the literature, painting and sculpture of white Americans: that is it shows more or less evidence of European influence."[344] He, like many of the conservative academicians, was

---

[343] David Levering Lewis, *When Harlem Was in Vogue*, 159.
[344] George Schuyler, *The Negro Art-Hokum*, 310.

embarrassed by racial stereotypes evident in the caricatures promulgated in much of the *Tin Pan Alley* music that was reminiscent of nineteenth-century minstrelsy. Schuyler agreed with Locke's theory that when artists create art that is strictly in the context of racial themes, they admit to an inability to create works that meet the standards of Western critics. The same critics possessed the power to affirm or deny the validity and quality of any art. Schuyler cleverly used satire to criticize the social efforts of both Harlem's elite community (who often produced formal balls and parties that were absent of popular jazz and blues music) as well as the affairs of the opposite populace who possessed considerably less disposable income. Those Harlemites often gave rent parties and frequented popular nightspots available to them.

Unfortunately, Locke and Schuyler ignored the mastery inherent in composers Eubie Blake and Noble Sissle's Broadway production, *Chocolate Dandies* and Edward "Duke" Ellington's neo-impressionistic composition, *Black and Tan Fantasy*. Both works of art were seminal to the period's culture. The former was the first black theatrical production performed on Broadway. In *Black and Tan Fantasy*, Ellington musically expounded on the possibilities of improvising blues music that is juxtaposed with the style of Harlem stride piano. The creation subsequently became a notable example of the composer's early compositional style.

Armstrong's place of birth, New Orleans, was integral to the development of American jazz music and the blues, and consequently the period's art. The enslaved Africans' cultural behavior, particularly their music performance practices in Congo Square manifested in the development of jazz. The musical approach of poly or stratified rhythms while harnessing the timbre of the instruments being played is embraced by the descendants (second and third generations) of the Congo Square musicians who were performing pre-Civil War. Theorist, Olly Wilson noted the similarities in West African music-making as it relates to African-American. He identified the utilization of poly-rhythms, call-response, a communal approach to making music, percussive body usage, and the presence of a heterogeneous sound ideal, in the performing of Ghanaian folk music. Wilson published his findings in a 1974 article titled, *The Relationship Between African-American and West African Music*.[345] The process of making music that Wilson described mirrored the music practices that were present in Congo Square. Wilson theorized that the earliest jazz musicians, who were one or two generations removed from Congo Square, used the same musical approach as their enslaved ancestors, but on European musical instruments.

Additionally, a textual analysis of eyewitness reports published by outsiders such as Benjamin Latrobe, who visited the area, reveals the presence of the West African musical practices identified by Wilson. Interestingly, Armstrong's collaborator on *Texas Moaner Blues* was early blues and jazz pioneer, Sidney Bechet's grandfather, Omar, a Congo Square musician. Bechet dedicated the second chapter of his autobiography, *Treat It Gentle* to disseminate his grandfather Omar's story. An analysis of a music transcription of the 1924 recording reveals the presence of the musical practices identified by Wilson and noted by Latrobe. Indeed, Armstrong and Bechet are less than a decade removed from New Orleans' cultural practices, particularly its blues tradition, specifically as it relates to the performing arts.

One of the salient aspects of blues music as well as the other Black American folk music traditions, from which it came, is the genre's functionality. Specifically, the music often meant one thing to the musician, and another to the consumer. There was the presence of an ingenious use of double-entendre, making the performing art function with a purpose beyond mere entertaining. Historically, the enslaved Africans developed a system of using double entendre to send messages of planned escapes. Songs such as *Swing Low Sweet Chariot*, *Deep River*, and *I'm Gonna Lay Down My Burdens*, had texts with double meanings. Former slave and abolitionist, Frederick Douglass surmised: "Slaves sing more to make themselves happy, than to express happiness." After describing a planned escape Douglass stated that "A keen observer might have detected in our repeated singing of 'O Canaan, sweet Canaan, I

---

[345] See Olly Wilson's "The Relationship Between African-American and West African Music" *Black Perspectives in Music* 2, no.1 (Spring 1974): 15-22.

am bound for the land of Canaan,' something more than a hope of reaching heaven. We meant to reach the north---and the north was our Canaan."[346] In both instances, the performing art had alternate functions from the perspective of the producer and the receiver. The enslaved used the music as a conduit for melancholy relief and affirmation of a planned escape respectively. Ingeniously, the music functioned as more than entertainment, but inconspicuous codes. Consumers often developed an affinity for the musical expressions of an oppressed group suffering from the horrors of the peculiar institution. All too often consumers of black art view it in the context of entertainment. This gave rise to an appropriation of such art. Specifically, minstrelsy, *Tin Pan Alley*, and Carl Van Vechten's fiction, *Nigger Heaven*.

Similarly, African-American post-Civil War performing art in the south functioned alternately for the producer and consumer. The system of sharecropping, as well as much of America's industrial production (railroads, steel, and military), inspired intensive labor tasks. The necessity of coordinating tasks as well as creating a coping mechanism was imperative. Consequently, the invention of field hollers was inevitable. To the observer or consumer, such performing art may have been entertaining as a vocal leader (usually hired because of ability to vocalize and improvise) phrases and elicits a response from his targeted co-workers. Thus, the creation of blues music was an outgrowth of the field hollers. It too functioned as a coping mechanism and just as the music of the enslaved; it provided a melancholy relief. The genre's role in the former is evident in many of the lyrics of early blues music.

Though the period preceded the invention of sound recording, one can get a glimpse of the performing art from the itinerant solo musicians that traversed the South just before and during the Harlem Renaissance. Songs like *See That My Grave Is Kept Clean* by "Blind Lemon Jefferson (discussed in Chapter IV) and *Sobin Heart Blues* by Bessie Smith are seminal examples of coping with inevitable or unavoidable death and a lost romantic love respectively. Additionally, the music served as a source

---

[346] Eileen Southern, *Readings in Black American Music* (New York: W. W. Norton and Co., 1983), 87.

of liberation as the producer often identified a problem (which initiates the process of freeing oneself from said social ills) and offered a solution.

The weight of this research was to document Louis Armstrong's and particular literary and visual artists, was done at the expense of not discussing the importance of other figures. For example, this researcher did not explore in any detail the impact of Marcus Garvey and the Universal Negro Improvement Association. Garvey attracted many African-Americans seeking relief from the oppressive conditions not only in the South but the urban North. Garvey's "back to Africa" admonitions in some instances created a binary result. It inspired thousands to collectively prepare a conduit for a mass exodus of black Americans back to Africa. Indeed, for many blacks, the U.N.I.A. was the first organization (beyond the black church) with specific plans, hierarchy, and infrastructure that embraced their African heritage. The group attracted thousands and indeed purchased a steam liner to begin the exodus. The other outgrowth of Garvey's theory was a psychological return to Africa. For many, particularly artists, Garvey's speeches and the U.N.I.A.'s presence along with the research and publications of Carter G. Woodson on African-American and African history as well as the research of Arnold Schoenberg, inspired a new at Africa as a contributor to world history.

One cannot underestimate the artistic contributions of Paul Robeson during the period considered here. Robeson's was an actor, orator, and vocalist. He performed weekly in theater and solo concerts. He also gained a reputation as an acclaimed stage actor. Similarly, this research did not discuss in detail the significant impact of period musicians, Sidney Bechet, Fats Waller, Edward "Duke" Ellington, and Fletcher Henderson. Each made notable contributions to the music of the Harlem Renaissance and the American music canon. Bechet was one of the first to bring the American art form to an international stage when he and Josephine Baker joined the Will Marion Cook Orchestra for a tour of Europe. One may argue that the success of James Reese Europe less than a decade earlier may have been the first to spread American folk music to an international stage.

Intense competition for piano jobs inspired the development of the "Harlem Stride" piano playing style. James P. Johnson and Willie "The Lion" Smith were the style's chief promulgators. The artists play a steady ostinato in several octaves and at fast tempos in the left hand. Simultaneously, the right hand rapidly pounds out melodies and improvises. The "Harlem Stride" playing style received an artistic boost when pianist Art Tatum arrived and introduced a virtuosic two-handed approach to playing melodies. Though Tatum was relatively late on the scene, his impact is indelible, particularly when placed in the context of the subsequent be-bop era.

Additionally, one cannot underestimate the artistic contributions of Paul Robeson during the period considered here. Equally documented are Robeson's contributions to the Harlem Renaissance as an orator and vocalist. He also gained a reputation as an acclaimed stage actor. Robeson was also a significant social activist in the labor movement. Similarly, this research did not discuss in detail the impact of period musicians, Sidney Bechet, Fats Waller, Edward "Duke" Ellington, and Fletcher Henderson. Each made significant contributions to the music of the Harlem Renaissance and the American music canon. Bechet was one of the first to bring the American art form to an international stage when he and Josephine Baker joined the Will Marion Cook Orchestra for a tour of Europe. One may argue that the success of James Reese Europe less than a decade earlier may have been the first to spread American folk music to an international stage. More importantly, Reese's regimental band's exploits during World War I, should not overshadow the extraordinary bravery of the black soldiers. Certainly, the French government recognized their contributions and awarded the entire regiment the highest honor it can bestow, the Croix de Guerre.

The nation's economy declined significantly during the decade after the 1929 stock market crash. The devastating effects of the period known as "The Great Depression" proved even worse for black Americans. It also hastened the end of the Harlem Renaissance. However, Louis Armstrong's contributions American music continued. He began the decade collaborating with "country" music icon, Jimmie Rodgers. Their version of *Blue Yoddle No.9* was significant in two ways. Black and white artists seldom if ever performed or recorded together (to the detriment of jazz and blues music's development among white musicians) and it was a creative merger of country and blues music that foretold the genre's role as an aquifer for most of twentieth-century American music.

In conclusion, this writer made a serious attempt to show the relationships between West African musical and cultural practices to the mores and folkways of New Orleans, particularly as Louis Armstrong experienced them. Beyond the advantage of also coming of age in the region, this writer discussed specific West African ethnic groups, such as the Senegambians, Ewe, Ibo, Bambara, Mande, Ndongo, and Wolof, that made salient contributions through their enslavement in the region. This is one of the aspects that I am most proud of, given the contemporary attempts to eliminate the dissemination of such information in schools.

Michael Decuir

APPENDIX A

SIGNIFICANT LOUIS ARMSTRONG RECORDINGS AS A BAND LEADER 1925–1930

1925

Louis Armstrong and His Hot Five. "Gut Bucket Blue." Written by Louis Armstrong (Recorded November 12 in Chicago, Illinois. OKeh).

1926

_____. "Heebie Jeebies", written by B. Atkins, recorded February 26 in Chicago, Illinois. Okeh.

_____. "Cornet Chop Suey", written by Louis Armstrong. Recorded February 26 in Chicago, Illinois. Okeh.

_____. "King of the Zulus" written by Lil Armstrong. Recorded June 23 in Chicago, Illinois.

_____. "Skat-Dat-De-Dat" written by Lil Hardin. Recorded November 16 in Chicago, Illinois. OKeh.

_____. "Big Butter and Egg Man" written by P. Venable and Louis Armstrong. Recorded November 16, 1926 in Chicago, Illinois. OKeh.

1927

Louis Armstrong and His Hot Seven. "Potato Head Blues", written by Louis Armstrong. Recorded May 10 in Chicago, Illinois. OKeh.

_____. "Weary Blues", written by Mathews. Recorded May 11, 1927 in Chicago, Illinois. OKeh.

_____. "Struttin' with Some Barbecue" written by Lil Hardin and D. Raye. Recorded December 9 in Chicago, Illinois. OKeh.

_____. "Hotter Than That" written by Lil Hardin. Recorded December 13 in Chicago, Illinois, OKeh.

_____. "Savoy Blues" written by E. Ory. Recorded December 13 in Chicago. Illinois. OKeh.

1928

_____. "West End Blues" written by Clarence Williams and Joe Oliver. Recorded June 28 in Chicago, Illinois. OKeh.

_____. "Basin Street Blues" written by S. Williams. Recorded December 4 in Chicago, Illinois. OKeh.

_____. "Beau Koo Jack" written by A. Hill, Louis Armstrong, W. Melrose, and Don Redman. Recorded December 5 in in Chicago, Illinois. OKeh.

Louis Armstrong and Earl Hines. "Weather Bird" written by Joe Oliver. Recorded December 5 in Chicago, Illinois. OKeh.

_____. "Tight like This" written by Curl. Recorded, December 12 in Chicago, Illinois. OKeh.

1929

_____. "Mahogany Hall Stomp" written by S. Williams. Recorded March 5 in New York City, New York. OKeh.

_____. "Ain't Misbehavin" written by A. Razaf, T. Waller, H. Brooks. Recorded July 19 in New York City, New York. OKeh.

_____. "Black and Blue" written by A Razaf and T. Waller. Recorded July 22 in New York City, New York. OKeh.

_____. "When You're Smiling" written by Fisher, Goodwin, Shay. Recorded September 11 in New York City, New York. OKeh.

_____. "St. Louis Blues" (alternate Take B) Written by W.C. Handy. Recorded December 13 in New York City, New York. Columbia.

APPENDIX B

SIGNIFICANT LOUIS ARMSTRONG RECORDINGS AS A SIDEMAN 1923–1930

1923

King Oliver's Creole Jazz Band, "Chimes Blues," written by Joe Oliver. Recorded in Richmond Indiana, April 6, A. Gennett.

_____. "Snake Rag," written by Joe Oliver. Recorded June 22, 1923, in Chicago, Illinois. OKeh.

_____. "Tears," written by Joe Oliver. Recorded October 25, 1923, in Chicago, Illinois. OKeh.

1924

Ma Rainey, "See, See Rider Blues," (Writer Unknown) Recorded October 16 in New York City, New York. Paramount.

_____. "Countin' the Blues," by Virginia Liston. Recorded October 16 in New York City, New York. Paramount.

_____. "You've Got the Right Key, But the Wrong Keyhole," written by Recorded October 17 in New York City, New York. Paramount.

Clarence Williams's Blue Five, "Texas Moaner Blues," written by Clarence Williams and F. Barnes. Recorded October 17 in New York City, New York. Okeh.

———. "Everybody Loves My Baby," written by J. Palmer and S. Williams, Recorded November 9, 1924, in New York City, New York. OKeh.

Josephine Beatty (pseudonym for Alberta Hunter), "Everybody Loves My Baby," written by J. Palmer, and S. Williams. Recorded November 6 in New York City, New York. Okeh.

———. "Texas Moaner Blues," written by Clarence Williams and F. Barnes. Recorded November 8 in New York City, New York. OKeh.

Fletcher Henderson and His Orchestra, "Naughty Man," written by C. Dixon, D. Redman, and S. Ward. Recorded November 14, in New York City, New York. Columbia.

Margeret Johnson accompanied by Clarence Williams's Blue Five, "Changeable Daddy of Mine," written by Wooding/Schaffer. Recorded November 25, in New York City, New York. OKeh.

Sippie Wallace, "Baby, I Can't Use You No More," recorded November 28 in New York City, New York. OKeh.

———. "Trouble Everywhere I Roam," recorded November 28 in New York City, New York. OKeh.

Maggie Jones, "Poor House Blues," recorded December 9 in New York City, New York. Columbia.

———. "Thunderstorm Blues," recorded December 10 in New York City, New York. Columbia.

_____. "Anybody Here Want To Try My Cabbage," written by Razaff/Waller/Dowell. Recorded December 10 in New York City, New York. Columbia.

_____. "Good Time Flat Blues," written by S. Williams. Recorded December 17 in New York City, New York. Columbia.

Josephine Beatty (pseudonym for Alberta Hunter) with Clarence Todd, "Cake Walking Babies From Home," Written by H. Troy, C. Williams, and C. Smith, recorded December 22 in New York City, New York. Gannett.

1925

Clara Smith, "Nobody Knows The Way I Feel This Morning," recorded January 7 in New York City, New York. Columbia.

_____. "Broken Busted Blues," Recorded January 7 in New York City, New York. Columbia.

Eva Taylor, "Cake Walking Babies From Home," by H. Troy, C. Willimas, C. Smith. Recorded January 8, in New York City, New York. OKeh.

_____. "Pickin' On Your Baby," written by Reynolds/James and recorded on January 8, in New York City, New York. OKeh.

Clarence Williams's Blue Five, "Cake Walking Babies (from Home)," written by Clarence Williams, C. Smith, and H. Troy, Recorded January 8, 1925 in New York, New York. OKeh.

_____. "Pickin' on Your Baby," written by Reynolds/James. Recorded January 8 in New York City, New York. OKeh.

Bessie Smith, "St. Louis Blues," written by W. C. Handy and recorded on January 14 in New York City, New York. Columbia.

_____. "Sobbin' Hearted Blues," written by Bradford/Laver/ Davis. Recorded January 14, in New York City, New York. Columbia.

Clarence Williams's Blue Five. "Papa De-Da-Da," written by W. Melrose and J. Oliver. Recorded May 10 in New York City, New York. Columbia.

Trixie Smith, "The World's Jazz Crazy And So Am I," Recorded Mar? in New York City, New York. PM.

Clara Smith, "Shipwrecked Blues," recorded April 3 in New York City, New York. Columbia.

_____. "Court House Blues," Recorded April 3 in New York City, New York. Columbia.

Bessie Smith, "Nashville Woman's Blues," recorded May 26 in New York, New York, Columbia.

The Southern Serenaders, "Alone at Last," written by Kahn/Fiorito. Recorded August 7 in New York City, New York. Harmony.

Fletcher Henderson and His Orchestra. "T. N. T.," written by E. Schoebel. Recorded October 21 in New York City, New York. Columbia.

Clarence Williams's Blue Five, "You Can't Shush Katie," written by White/Creamer/Warren. Recorded October 26 in New York City, New York. OKeh.

Bertha "Chippie" Hill, "Low Land Blues," written by L. Nichols. Recorded November 9. in Chicago, Illinois. OKeh.

1926

Bertha "Chippie" Hill, "Lonesome All Alone and Blue," recorded February 23, 1926 in Chicago Illinois, OKeh.

Sippie Wallace, "A Jealous Woman like Me," recorded March 1, 1926, in Chicago, Illinois, OKeh.

Erskine Tate's Vendome Orchestra. "Stomp Off, Let's Go," written by Schoebel. Recorded May 28 in Chicago, Illinois. Vocallion.

Bertha "Chippie" Hill. "Pleadin' for the Blues" (unknown writer). Recorded November 23 in Chicago, Illinois. OKeh.

_____. "Lonesome Weary Blues," recorded November 26, 1926, in Chicago, Illinois, OKeh 8453.

1927

Johnny Dodds's Black Bottom Stompers. "Wild Man Blues," written by Morton/Armstrong. Recorded April 22 in Chicago, Illinois. Brunswick.

Sippie Wallace, "Dead Drunk Blues," recorded May 6, 1927, in Chicago, Illinois, OKeh 8499.

_____. "The Flood Blues" by Recorded May 6, 1927, in Chicago, Illinois, OKeh 8470.

1929

Seger Ellis, "Ain't Misbehavin," written by Fats Waller. Recorded August 26, 1928 in New York City, New York. OKeh.

1930

Jimmie Rodgers, "Blue Yodel No. 9," by Jimmie Rodgers. Recorded July 16, 1930, in Los Angeles, California, mx. W 403896-D, OKeh 41415.

1928

Lillie Delk Christian. "Too Busy," written by Miller/Cohn. Recorded May 26 in Chicago, Illinois. OKeh.

BIBLIOGRAPHY

Adorno, Theodor. "On Popular Music." *Cultural Theory and Popular Culture*. Fourth Edition. Edited by John Storey. London: Pearson, Longman, 2009.

Anderson, James D. *The Education of Blacks in the South, 1860–1935*. Chapel Hill: The University of North Carolina Press, 1988.

Armstrong, Louis. *Satchmo: My Life in New Orleans*. New York: DaCapo Press, 1954.

———. *Louis Armstrong: In His Own Words, Selected Writings* Thomas Brothers ed., (New York: Oxford University Press, 1999) 37.

———. *Swing That Music*. New York. DaCapo Press Centennial Edition. 1993.

Baker Jr., Houston A. *Blues, Ideology and Afro-American Literature: A Vernacular Theory*. Chicago: The University of Chicago Press, 1984.

———. *Modernism and the Harlem Renaissance*. Chicago: The University of Chicago Press, 1987.

Bakri, Al. "The Book of Routes and Realms." *Corpus of Early Arabic Sources for West Africa*. New York: Marcus Weiner Press, 1981.

Baraka, Amiri. *Blues People: Negro Music in White America.* St. Louis. Progressive Music Co.,1963.

Bauerlein, Mark. *Negrophobia: A Race Riot in Atlanta,1906.* San Francisco: Encounter Books. 2001.

Bay, Mia. Forward to "The Lighter of Truth: Writings of an Anti-Lynching Crusader. Ida B. Wells." Edited by Mia Bay and Henry Louis Gates, Jr. New York: Penguin Books, 2008.

Bearden, Romare. "The Negro Artist and Modern Art." *Opportunity* (December 1934): 37.

Bechet, Sidney. *Treat It Gentle.* New York: DeCapo Press, 1978. Blacking, John. *How Musical Is Man?* Seattle: The University of Washington Press, 1973. Brothers, Thomas. *Louis Armstrong's New Orleans.* New York: W.W. Norton, 2006.

Brown, Sterling. "Ma Rainey." *The Collected Poems of Sterling A. Brown.* Edited by Michael Harper. Evanston, IL: Northwestern University Press, 1980.

_____. "Memphis Blues." *The Collected Poems of Sterling Brown* ed. Michael Harper. Evanston, IL: Northwestern University, 1980.

Buckingham, Will. "Louis Armstrong and the Waif's Home." *The Jazz Archivist* XXIV (2011): 2–15.

Burns, Ken, Lynn Novick, Geoffrey C. Ward, Keith David, and Wynton Marsalis. *Jazz: A Film by Ken Burns.* [Alexandria, Va.]: PBS Home Video, 2004.

Caldwell, Charles. *Introductory Address on The Independence of Intellect,* 1825.

Coleman, Rick. *Blue Monday: Fats Domino and The Lost Dawn of Rock N' Roll.* New York: DaCapo Press. 2006.

Cooper, John Milton Jr. *Woodrow Wilson: A Biography.* New York: Vintage Books. 2011.

Cullen, Countee. "Yet Do I Marvel." *Color.* New York: Harper & Bros., 1925.

Cutler, James Elbert. *Lynch-Law: An Investigation into the History of Lynching in the United States.* New York: Longmans, Green, and Co., 1905.

Dewey, John. *Art as Experience.* New York: Capricorn Books, 1959. New York.

Diepeveen, Leonard. "Folktales in the Harlem Renaissance." *American Literature* 58, no. 1 (March 5, 1986): 64–81.

Diop, Cheike Ante. *Pre-Colonial Black Africa.* Chicago: Lawrence Hill Books, 1987.

Douglass, Frederick. *My Bondage and My Freedom.* New York: Miller, Orton & Mulligan, 1855.

Du Bois, W. E. B. *The Autobiography of W. E. B. DuBois: A Soliloquy on Viewing My Life from the Last Decade of the First Century.* New York: International Publishers Co., Inc., 1968.

_____. "The Conversation of the Races." *A W. E. B. Du Bois Reader.* Edited by Andrew G. Paschal. New York: Macmillan, 1971.

_____. "The Criteria of Negro Art." *Crisis Magazine* (October 1926): 10–11.

_____. *Efforts for Social Betterment among Negro Americans.* Atlanta: Atlanta University Press, 1910.

_____. "Returning Soldiers." *The Crisis Magazine* 18, no.1 (May, 1919): 14.

———. *The Souls of Black Folk.* New York: Barnes and Noble Classics, 2003.

Dunbar, Paul Lawrence. *The Death Song.* New York: Dodd, Mead and Company, 1913.

———. *When Malindy Sings.* New York: Dodd, Mead and Company, 1898.

Dyja, Thomas. *Walter White: The Dilemma of Black Identity in America.* Chicago: Ivan R. Dee, 2008.

Erskine, Gilbert M. "'Countin' the Blues: A Survey of the Recordings Of Louis Armstrong Accompanying Singers in the 1920s." *The Second Line.* New Orleans: Hogan Jazz Archives. Tulane University (Spring 1976): 10–19.

Europe, James Reese. "The Negro Explains Jazz." *Literary Digest.* (April 26, 1919): 28–29.

Evans, David. "Techniques of Blues Composition among Black Folksingers." *Journal of American Folklore Society* 87, no. 345 (Jul-Sep. 1974): 240–49.

Fanon, Franz. *The Wretched of the Earth.* New York: Grove Press, 1963.

Finkelstein, Sidney. *Jazz: A People's Music.* New York: DaCapo Press. 1975.

Fisher, Rudolph. "The Caucasian Storms Harlem." *American Mercury.* August 1927.

Floyd Jr., Samuel. *The Power of Black Music.* New York: Oxford University Press, 1995.

Frazier, Edward Franklin. "La Bourgeoisie Noir." *The Portable Harlem Renaissance Reader*. Edited by David Levering Lewis. New York: Penguin Books, 1994.

Friere, Paulo. *Pedagogy of the Oppressed*. London: Penguin Books, 1993.

Gabbin, Joanne V. *Sterling Brown: Building the Black Aesthetic Tradition*. Charlottesville: University of Virginia Press, 1985.

Garvey, Marcus. *Africa for Africans*. New York: Routledge, Taylor, and Francis Group, 1923.

Giddins, Paula J. *Ida: A Sword among Lions*. New York: Harper Collins Publishers, 2008.

Grout, Donald Jay. *A History of Western Music*. New York: Norton, 1960.

Hall, Gwendolyn Midlo. *Africans in Colonial Louisiana: The Development of Afro-Creole Culture in the Eighteenth Century*. Baton Rouge: Louisiana State University Press, 1992.

Handy, William Christopher. "The Heart of the Blues." *Etude Music Magazine* (March 1940): 152,193–194.

Hart, Robert C. "Black-White Literary Relations in the Harlem Renaissance." *American Literature* 44, no. 4 (Jan. 1973): 612–28.

Hitler, Adolph. *Mein Kampf*. Translated by Ralph Manheim. Boston: Houghton Mifflin Company, 1998.

Hoffer, Charles. *Music Listening Today*. Belmont CA: Thomson Learning, 2003.

Holley, Joseph W. *You Can't Build a Chimney from the Top*. Lanham, MD: University Press of America, 1948.

Hobson, Vic. *Louis Armstrong and Barbershop Harmony: Creating the Jazz Solo.* Jackson: University Press of Mississippi. 2018.

Huggins, Nathan W. "Visual Arts: To Celebrate Blackness." *Voices from the Harlem Renaissance.* Edited by Nathan W. Huggins. New York: Oxford University Press, 1995, 259–61.

Hughes, Langston. "Blues Fantasy." *The Collected Poems of Langston Hughes.* Edited by Arnold Rampersad and David Roessel. New York: Vintage Books, 1995.

———. "Jazzonia." *The Collected Poems of Langston Hughes.* Edited by Arnold Rampersad and David Roessel. New York: Vintage Books, 1995.

———. "The Negro Artist and the Racial Mountain." *The Nation* CXXII (June 1926): 290-297.

———. "The Negro Speaks of Rivers." *Selected Poems.* New York: Alfred Knopf, Inc., 1926.

———. "Weary Blues." *Selected Poems.* New York: Alfred A. Knopf, Inc., 1926.

Hurston, Zora Neal. *Mules and Men.* Philadelphia: J. B. Lippincott, 1935.

———. *Their Eyes Were Watching God.* Philadelphia: J.B. Lippincott, 1937.

Hutchinson, George. *The Harlem Renaissance in Black and White.* Cambridge: Harvard University Press, 1995.

Jackson, George G. *Introduction to African Civilizations.* New York: Carol Publishing Group, 1970.

Jackson, L. A. *Musicology 2101: A Quick Start Guide to Music Biz History*. Edited by Anna R. Holloway. Atlanta: MKM Publishing, 2012.

Jackson, Mahalia. *Movin On Up*. New York: Hawthorn Books, 1966.

Johnson, Charles. "The Negro Renaissance and its Significance." *The New Negro Thirty Years Afterward*. Washington, DC: Howard University Press, 1955.

Johnson, Fenton. "The Banjo Player." From *The Book of American Negro Poetry*. New York: Harcourt and Brace Co., 1922.

Johnson, James Weldon. *The Book of American Negro Poetry*. First Edition. New York: Harcourt and Brace Co., 1922.

_____. "The Color Sergeant." *Fifty Years and Other Poems*. Boston: The Cornhill Co., 1917.

_____. "The Making of Harlem." *Survey Graphic Magazine* (March, 1925): 635-639.

_____. "God's Trombones." New York: Viking Press, 1927.

_____. "O Black and Unknown Bards." *Saint Peter Relates An Incident*. New York: Penguin Books, 191.

Jones, Joseph. "Interview by George W. Kay." *Hogan Jazz Archives*. New Orleans: Tulane University, 1974.

Kay, George W. Forward to "Louis Armstrong's Letter to His Daddy." *The Second Line Bicentennial Issue*. Hogan Jazz Archives. Tulane University, 1976.

King, J. *The Biology of Race*. Los Angeles: University of California Press, 1981.

Kirschke, Amy. *Aaron Douglas: Art, Race, and the Harlem Renaissance.* Jackson: The University of Mississippi Press, 1995.

Kmen, Henry. *Music in New Orleans.* Baton Rouge: Louisiana State University Press, 1966.

Latrobe, Benjamin. *Journal of Latrobe.* New York: D. Appleton, 1905.
Leary, Joy DeGruy. *Post Traumatic Slave Syndrome.* Milwaukie, OR: Upton Press, 2005.

Lewis, David Levering. *W. E. B. DuBois, The Fight for Equality and the American Century, 1919-1963.* New York: Henry Holt and Company, 2000.

_____. *The Portable Harlem Renaissance Reader.* Edited by David Levering Lewis. New York: Penguin Books, 1996.

_____. *When Harlem Was in Vogue.* New York: Penguin Books, 1997.

_____. "The Intellectual Luminaries of the Harlem Renaissance." *The Journal of Blacks in Higher Education,* no. 7 (Spring 1995): 68–69.

Locke, Alain. "Art or Propaganda." *Harlem* Vol. 1 (November 1928): 219, 256.

_____. "The Legacy of the Ancestral Arts." *The New Negro.* New York: Atheneum Publishers, 1925.

_____. "The New Negro." *The New Negro.* New York: Atheneum Publishers, 1925.

Locke, David. *Worlds of Music: An Introduction to the Music of the World's Peoples.*

Third Edition. Editors by Timothy Cooley, David Locke, David P. McAllester, Anne K. Rasmussen, David B. Reck, John M. Schecter,

Jonathan. P. J. Stock, R. Anderson Sutton. Belmont, CA: Schimer Cengage Learning, 2009).

Loggins, Vernon. *Where the World Ends.* Baton Rouge: Louisiana State University Press. 1958.

Machlis, Joseph and Forney, Kristine. *The Enjoyment of Music: An Introduction to Perceptive Listening.* New York: W.W. Norton & Co., 2003.

Marquis, Donald. *In Search of Buddy Bolden.* Baton Rouge: Louisiana State University Press, 1978.

Marsalis, Branford. *Jazz: A Film by Ken Burns.* Episode One. *Gumbo* [Alexandria, Va.]: PBS Home Video 2000.

McKay, Claude. "If We Must Die." Edited by David Levering Lewis. *The Portable Harlem Renaissance Reader.* New York: Penguin Books, 1994.

_____. "The New Negro in Paris," *A Long Way Home.* The Archives of Claude McKay, 1928.

Megill, Donald D. and Richard S. Demory. *Introduction to Jazz History.* Englewood Cliffs, CA: Prentice-Hall, Inc., 1984.

Mendy, Greer E. *Black Dance in Louisiana, Guardian of a Culture.* (New Orleans: Tekrema Center for African Diaspora Cultural Literacy, 2017) 11.

Miller, Geoffrey. *The Mating Mind.* New York: Anchor Books, 2001.

Morgenstern, Dan. "Louis Armstrong." *Companion to Jazz.* Edited by B. Kirchner. New York: Oxford University Press, 2000.

Park, Mongo. *The Journal of a Mission to the Interior of Africa in the Year 1805*. London: John Murray, 1815.

Patterson, James H. Forward to *The Healing Properties of the Blues: Moaning, Mourning. Morning,* Sandra Foster, 2020 Library of Congress Control Number: 2019921208

Peress, Maurice. *Dvorak to Duke Ellington: A Conductor Explores American Music and Its African American Roots*. Oxford: Oxford University Press, 2004.

Philipson, Robert. "The Harlem Renaissance as Postcolonial Phenomenon." *African American Review* 40, no. 1 (Spring, 2006): 145.

Porter, Bob. "Blues in Jazz." *The Oxford Companion to Jazz*. Edited by B. Kirchner. New York: Oxford University Press, 2000.

Porter, Lewis and Greg Ullman. "Sidney Bechet and His Long Song." *Black Perspectives in Music* 16, no.2. (1989): 140.

Rampersad, Arnold. "The Book That Launched the Harlem Renaissance." *The Journal of Blacks in Higher Education*, no. 38 (Winter, 2002-2003): 87–91.

_____. Forward to *Harlem Renaissance*. Nathan Irvin Huggins. New York: Oxford University Press. 2007.

Randolph, Asa Phillip. New Crowd—New Negro. *The Messenger* (May–June, 1919).

Rasmussen, David. *American Uprising: The Untold Story of America's Largest Slave Revolt*. New York: Harper Collins, 2011.

Schier, Helga. *George Washington Carver: Agricultural*. Edina, Minnesota: ABDO Publishing Co. 2008.

Schomburg, Arturo. "The Negro Digs Up His Past." *Voices from the Harlem Renaissance*. Edited by Nathan Irvin Huggins. New York: Oxford University Press, 1976.

Schuyler, George. *Black and Conservative: The Autobiography of George Schuyler*. New York: Arlington House Publishers, 1966.

_____. "The Negro Art-Hokum." *The Nation*, June, 1926.

_____. "Our Greatest Gift to America." *Anthology of American Negro Literature*. Edited by C. V. Calverton. New York: Alfred A. Knopf, Inc., 1929.

Sertima, Ivan Van. *They Came Before Columbus: The African Presence in Ancient America*. New York: Random House, 1976.

Shaw, Arthel. *Jazz: A Film* by Ken Burns. Episode Three. The Gift. [Alexandria, Va.]: PBS Home Video 2000.

Smock, Raymond W. *Booker T. Washington: Black Leadership in the Age of Jim Crow*. Chicago: Ivan R. Dee Publisher, 2009.

Somé, Malidoma Patrice. *The Healing Wisdom of Africa: Finding Life Purpose Through Nature, Ritual, and Community*. New York: Jeremy P. Tarcher/Putnam, 1998.

Southern, Eileen. *The Music of Black Americans*. New York: W.W. Norton & Co., 1997.

Sublette, Ned. *The World That Made New Orleans: From Spanish Silver to Congo Square*. Chicago: Lawrence Hill Books, 2009.

Tavernier, Bertrand. *Jazz: A Film* by Ken Burns. Episode Seven. Dedicated to Chaos. [Alexandria, Va.]: PBS Home Video 2000.

Taylor, Malesha. Discussion at The Institute of Black Intellectual Innovation Conference. *Innovating Sounds: Sonic Resistance and Ray Charles.* April 20, 2021.

Teachout, Terry. *Pops: A Life of Louis Armstrong.* Boston: Houghton Mifflin Harcourt, 2009.

Tkweme, W.S. "Blues in Stereo: The Texts of Langston Hughes in Jazz Music." *African American Review* 42, no.3 (Fall-Winter, 2008): 503–12.

Titon, Jeff Todd., *Worlds of Music: An Introduction into the Music of the World's Peoples.* Third Edition, Edited by Jeff Todd Titon, Timothy Cooley, David Locke. David P. McAllester, et al. Boston: Cengage Learning, 2009).

Townsend, Henry. Quoted in Houston Baker Jr., *Blues, Ideology and Afro-American Literature: A Vernacular Theory.* Chicago: The University of Chicago Press, 1984.

Van Vechten, Carl. *Nigger Heaven.* Chicago: University of Illinois Press, 2000.

Wald, Elijah. *Escaping the Delta: Robert Johnson and the Invention of the Blues.* New York: Harper Collins Books, 2004.

Washington, Booker T. *Up from Slavery.* New York: Signet Classic, 2000.

Waters, Ethel and Charles Samuels. *His Eye Is on the Sparrow.* New York: Doubleday & Co., 1950.

Wells, Ida Barnett. *Crusade for Justice: The Autobiography of Ida B. Wells.* Chicago: The University of Chicago Press, 1970.

_____. "The Truth About Lynching." New York: New York Age, 1892.

Wilson, Olly. "The Significance of the Relationship Between Afro-American Music and West African Music." *Black Perspectives in Music* 2, no.1 (Spring, 1974): 15–22.

Winz, Cary. "The Harlem Renaissance, 1920-1940: The Critics and the Harlem Renaissance Vol. 4." *African American Review* 32, no. 3 (Autumn 1998): 495–97.

Woodson, Carter G. "The Migration of the Talented Tenth." *A Century of Negro Migration*. New York: Dover Publications, 1918.

———. *The Mis-Education of the Negro*. Mineola, NY: Dover Publications, 1933.

———. *The Negro in Our History*. Washington DC: The Associated Publishers. Inc., 1922.

Wright, Richard. "The Blueprint for Negro Writing." *The Portable Harlem Renaissance Reader,* Edited by David Levering Lewis, New York: Penguin Books, 1994. West African Music." *Black Perspectives in Music* 2, no.1 (Spring, 1974): 15–22.

Winz, Cary. "The Harlem Renaissance, 1920-1940: The Critics and the Harlem Renaissance Vol. 4." *African American Review* 32, no. 3 (Autumn. 1998): 495–97.

Woodson, Carter G. "The Migration of the Talented Tenth." *A Century of Negro Migration*. New York: Dover Publications, 1918.

———. *The Mis-Education of the Negro*. Mineola, NY: Dover Publications, 1933.

———. *The Negro in Our History*. Washington DC: The Associated Publishers. Inc., 1922.

ABOUT THE AUTHOR

Dr. Michael Decuir is a native of New Orleans, Louisiana, and currently serves as the Interim Chair of the Music Department, Director of University Bands at Clark Atlanta University where he teaches Woodwind Studies, Marching and Symphonic Bands, Conducting, Jazz History, and the History of African American Music. His coming of age in his hometown serves as one of the key factors that inspired him to research the impact of Louis Armstrong on the Harlem Renaissance. He has shared his research on Armstrong at various conferences. He often serves as the guest clinician for many honor and marching band camps. He has served in the field of Music Education for the past thirty-one years and has earned a reputation for successfully developing secondary and collegiate band programs. He earned a BA in Music Education from Southern University at New Orleans, MA in Music, from The University of California, Berkeley, and a Doctor of Arts in Humanities from Clark Atlanta University. He is also a performing blues, jazz, and classical artist. His primary instruments are alto and tenor saxophones, clarinet, and flute. He enjoys the reputation as a caring teacher concerned with student achievement and successful educational experiences. He is the Music Director of the Southern Art Music Ensemble, a member of the Atlanta Soul Symphony Orchestra, and The Southernaires Jazz Band.

www.ingramcontent.com/pod-product-compliance
Lightning Source LLC
LaVergne TN
LVHW041804060526
838201LV00046B/1115